A Nation of Moochers

A Nation of
MOOCHERS

America's Addiction
to Getting
Something for Nothing

Charles J. Sykes

ST. MARTIN'S PRESS 〽 NEW YORK

www.stmartins.com

Design by Mspace/Maura Fadden Rosenthal

Library of Congress Cataloging-in-Publication Data

Sykes, Charles J., 1954–
    A nation of moochers : America's addiction to getting something for nothing / Charles J. Sykes. — 1st ed.
        p.   cm.
    ISBN 978-0-312-54770-7 (hardcover)
    ISBN 978-1-4299-5107-4 (e-book)
    1. Public welfare—United States.   2. Subsidies—United States. 3. United States—Social policy—1993–   4. United States—Economic policy—2009–   I. Title.
    HV95.S95 2012
    361.6'50973—dc23

                                                    2011036244

First Edition: January 2012

10 9 8 7 6 5 4 3 2 1

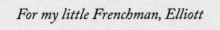

For my little Frenchman, Elliott

Contents

CONTENTS

Preface

Mooch: verb—*he was always mooching money from us:* beg, ask for money, borrow; *informal:* scrounge, bum, sponge, cadge.
noun—*she is such a mooch:* beggar; *informal:* bum, scrounger, cadger, freeloader, moocher.

(*Oxford American Writer's Thesaurus*)

Why "moochers"?

The title of this book could have been *Tin Cup Nation*, or *A Nation of Freeloaders*. This could have been a book about "dependency" or the "culture of entitlement."

But "moocher"—in all its anachronistic glory—perfectly captures the new culture of bailouts and irresponsible grasping, everything from corporations feeding at the trough to the permanent "victims" of Hurricane Katrina. Appropriately pejorative and judgmental, "moocher" is so old, it is fresh again. What it lacks in sophistication, it more than makes up for with its bracing bluntness. The next time you are at a cocktail party and a corporate CEO brags about his latest bit of government pork, try responding: "In other words, you are a moocher." You may ruin the party, but you will have effectively cut through an awful lot of euphemism and rationalization.

Befitting the times, "moocher" is already making a comeback. Ayn Rand's use of "moochers and looters" has gained new currency in the era of the Tea Party. Humorist P. J. O'Rourke titled his paean to Tax Day 2009 "A Nation of Moochers"[1]; syndicated talk-show host Neal Boortz has both talked and written extensively about the "moocher class"; and *Forbes* magazine recently introduced what it called the "moocher ratio" to measure the degree of dependence on government.[2] I hope this book will make a modest contribution in restoring the word to its rightful place in the American lexicon.

Part One

MOOCHER NATION

Scenes from Moocher Nation

✷　✷　✷

Mankind soon learns to make interested uses of every right and power which they possess or may assume. The public money and public liberty . . . will soon be discovered to be sources of wealth and dominion to those who hold them; distinguished, too, by this tempting circumstance: that they are the instrument as well as the object of acquisition. With money we will get men, said Caesar, and with men we will get money. . . . [Our] assembly should look forward to the time, and that not a distant one, when a corruption in this, as in the country from which we derive our origin, will have seized the heads of government, and be spread by them through the body of the people; when they will purchase the voices of the people, and make them pay the price.

—Thomas Jefferson, *Notes on Virginia*, 1782

✷　✷　✷

Q: Why are you here?
A: To get some money.
Q: What kind of money?
A: Obama money.
Q: Where's it coming from?

A: Obama.

Q: And where did Obama get it?

A: I don't know, his stash. . . . I don't know; I don't know where he got it from. But's he giving it to us. To help us. We love him. That's why we voted for him.

> —Detroit, October 7, 2009, where thousands of residents turned out for free government money. According to the Associated Press, they were supposed to apply for federal antihomelessness grants, but many were under the impression they were registering for $3,000 checks from the Obama administration.

✳   ✳   ✳

At the meeting, it was hard to discern where concerns over AIG's collapse ended and concern for Goldman Sachs began: Among the 40 or so people in attendance, Goldman Sachs was on every side of the large conference table, with "triple" the number of representatives as other banks, says another person who was there. . . .

The Goldman domination of the meetings might not have raised eyebrows if a private solution had been forthcoming. . . .

Of the $52 billion paid to AIG's counterparties, Goldman Sachs was the biggest recipient: $13 billion, the entire balance of its claim.

> —*New York* magazine[1]

✳ ✳ ✳

On Wednesday, 30,000 people suffered through hours in the hot sun, angry flare-ups in the crowd and lots of frustration and confusion for a chance to receive a government-subsidized apartment.

The massive event sometimes descended into a chaotic mob scene filled with anger and impatience.

—*The Atlanta Journal-Constitution*[2]

✳ ✳ ✳

At 300 East 23rd Street in the exclusive Gramercy Park neighborhood of Manhattan, a new 98-unit luxury apartment complex has been built with an outdoor movie theater and panoramic city views. The problem is that not enough buyers are coughing up the $820,000 to $3 million the project's developers are asking for the privilege to own a unit in the building. . . . Last December, the Federal Housing Administration loosened its financing rules so that U.S. taxpayers would have the honor of backing loans with down payments as low as 3.5%. Now rich Manhattanites can better afford condos in buildings with pet spas, concierges and rooftop lounges like the one in Gramercy Park, all on the taxpayers' dime.

—The Heritage Foundation[3]

＊ ＊ ＊

More than $69 million in California welfare money, meant to help the needy pay their rent and clothe their children, has been spent or withdrawn outside the state in recent years, including millions in Las Vegas, hundreds of thousands in Hawaii and thousands on cruise ships sailing from Miami.

—*Los Angeles Times*[4]

＊ ＊ ＊

In Wilkinson County, Miss., a home has been flooded 34 times since 1978. . . .

The home's value is $69,900. Yet the total insurance payments are nearly 10 times that: $663,000. . . .

The insurer? The federal government. . . .

In Fairhope, Ala., the owner of a $153,000 house has received $2.3 million in claims. A $116,000 Houston home has received $1.6 million.

—*USA Today*[5]

＊ ＊ ＊

A federal program designed to help impoverished families heat and cool their homes wasted more than $100 million paying the electric bills of thousands of applicants who were dead, in prison or living in million-dollar mansions, according to a government investigation. . . .

Illinois paid $840 toward energy bills for a U.S. Postal Service employee who fraudulently reported zero income even though she earned about $80,000 per year.

"Times are tough and I needed the money," she told investigators.

—Associated Press[6]

✻　✻　✻

El Campo, Tex.—Even though Donald R. Matthews put his sprawling new residence in the heart of rice country, he is no farmer. . . . Yet under a federal agriculture program approved by Congress, his 18-acre suburban lot receives about $1,300 in annual "direct payments," because years ago the land was used to grow rice.

Matthews is not alone. Nationwide, the federal government has paid at least $1.3 billion in subsidies for rice and other crops since 2000 to individuals who do no farming at all. . . .

—*The Washington Post*[7]

Chapter 1

A NATION OF MOOCHERS

We are all born moochers; whether we choose to remain so determines our character and our future. All we have to lose is our dependency.

Is America becoming a country where the irresponsible and grasping increasingly live off of those who work, save, invest, and otherwise play by the rules? Have we reached a tipping point where more Americans are relying on the efforts of others rather than their own?

Are we becoming a nation of moochers?

We are very close to that point if we have not already crossed the line. From the corporate bailouts on Wall Street to the declining stigmas on default and dependency, the new moocher culture cuts across lines of class, race, and private and public sectors.

Members of the middle class are increasingly as likely to become moochers as the poor; CEOS are as likely to belly up to the trough as the underprivileged; and the BlackBerry has emerged as a more effective tool for mooching than a tin cup. In the Great Bailout, an expensively educated, richly compensated, elaborately insulated, politically powerful, and well-connected elite toyed with the nation's wealth and bailed themselves out at the expense of millions of waitresses, steamfitters, shopkeepers, schoolteachers, farmers, retirees—and their children and grandchildren—in what may turn out to be the greatest intergenerational transfer of wealth in history.

Momentum

Moocher Nation is not driven by a coherent ideology or even a consistent approach to dealing with either need or "fairness." What it has is . . . momentum.

More programs of dependency generate more reliance on ever more and varied handouts, as the habit of dependency becomes ingrained and increasingly attractive to others. Subsidies breed subsidies; pork inspires pork (especially if it can masquerade as stimulus); tax credits multiply like bacteria; and lobbyists swarm at the prospect of congressional handouts. The explosion of bailouts and handouts creates its own dynamic: How can you say no to would-be moocher A when B and C are getting mountains of federal cash? How can politicians turn down farmers when the bankers are fattening at the trough; or plead for fiscal restraint to Main Street when Wall Street is awash in OPM (Other People's Money)? One CEO who jumps on a Gulfstream jet to fly to Washington to wring a few billion dollars from compliant senators inspires dozens, maybe hundreds, of other businessmen to book planes, trains, and limousines to get their own slice of somebody else's American Dream.

The stigma of dependency—being on the dole—still runs deep in American culture, certainly far deeper than in Great Britain or France, where students and pensioners take to the streets at the merest whiff of a suggestion that they might lose one of their cherished benefits. But it is not inexhaustible. The stigma has been all but erased in some central cities where the long lines that form even at the rumor of free stuff have become testaments to the pervasiveness of the moocher culture, a way of life passed from generation to generation.

Meanwhile, the infrastructure of mooching issues forth armies of social workers, caring professionals, caseworkers, program officers, bureaucrats, advocates, activists, and nonprofits, who see it as their mission to ease the transition of taxpayer dollars into the hands of the "disadvantaged," or at least the well-connected. Every crisis, every natural disaster or financial setback, becomes another occasion for expanding the size of the moocher state. Each cause has its own symbols of need and woe and justification for their own comfortable jobs as agents of the moocher culture: the deprived child, the bereft farmer, the impoverished oldster—but the message is always the same: more. Says the Tax Foundation's Scott Hodge: "Every marketing guru will tell you that people love free stuff and they will take as much as they can get whether they need it or not. But for a nation, this is a recipe for disaster."[1]

Human nature being what it is, politicians throughout the ages have understood that it is far easier and more popular to hand out bread and circuses, entitlements, and freebies than it is to take them away. Promises, even if they are unaffordable, tend to win more votes than truth telling, especially if that means delivering the bad news that there is no more free lunch and that government workers might have to contribute more to their own pensions.

Scenes of public employees besieging state capitols in Wisconsin and Ohio to protect their bloated benefits and union power are likely a preview of the ferocity with which the entitled will fight to keep their spot at the public trough.

Always More

There is an inexorable quality to the new culture. Regardless of how much has already been done or whether those efforts have succeeded or failed, advocates continue to press for ever greater efforts by the government to help the downtrodden. By definition, whatever has been or is being or will be done is insufficient: After trillions of dollars spent on the War on Poverty, more is urgently required, even if that means continually redefining poverty. But it is one thing to erect a safety net for the needy, and quite another to provide a soft down-filled mattress with a taxpayer-funded mint on the pillow and minibar privileges.

Some of these developments can be dismissed as artifacts of the deep recession, but the loss of the stigma associated with default and dependency may also mark a decisive shift in the American ethos and character. The Great Recession of 2007 saw the destruction of millions of jobs and vastly increased the numbers of Americans reliant on government. But the growth in dependency predated the deluge and Washington used the crisis as a pretext to further shrink the private sector and expand government dependency. This recession hit hardest those who played by the rules and sharpened the gap between the two Americas: those who had 401(k)s, owned a home they intended to pay for, and worked in the private economy, versus those who lived on government entitlements, deadbeats who defaulted on debts, and companies that benefited from bailouts or massive pork subsidies. All of this raises fundamental issues of fairness. As Oxford University ethicist Henry Shue says, "If whoever makes a mess receives the benefits and does not pay the costs, not only does he have no incentive to avoid making as many messes as he likes, but he is also unfair to whoever does pay the costs." And philosopher David Schmidtz explains, "To be just is to avoid, as best we can, leaving our neighbors to pay for our negligent choices."[2]

But that is precisely what has happened. Much of the anger of recent years stems from the realization by millions of Americans that the story of the ant and the grasshopper is being turned on its head: Increasingly, those who take responsibility are being asked to bail out the profligate.

The milestones are troubling:

- Even as more people became dependent on government, fewer were paying their share of the tab. By tax day in 2010, nearly half of U.S. households paid no federal income taxes. After years of cuts, credits, and outright rebates, 47 percent of households had no net liability at all. A family of four could make up to $51,000 without paying a nickel in federal income taxes.[3] Many of them have a "negative tax liability," which means they get a check from the government.

  "The result," notes the Associated Press, "is a tax system that exempts almost half the country from paying for programs that benefit everyone, including national defense, public safety, infrastructure, and education."[4]

- While the top 10 percent of earners now pay around 73 percent of the federal income tax burden, fully 40 percent of individuals actually get more money from the tax system than what they pay in. Rather than sending in a tax payment on April 15, the government actually sends them a check, paid for, of course, by other taxpayers. "In essence," writes the Tax Foundation's Hodge, "lawmakers have turned the IRS into an ATM machine for welfare benefits—and ATM now stands for Another Taxpayer's Money."[5]

• There are now more takers than makers in the American economy. As *The Wall Street Journal*'s Stephen Moore writes, in the United States today, government now employs nearly twice as many people (22.5 million) as work in all of manufacturing (11.5 million). "It gets worse," notes Moore. "More Americans work for the government than work in construction, farming, fishing, forestry, manufacturing, mining and utilities combined. We have moved decisively from a nation of makers to a nation of takers."[6]

• Reliance on government has hit an all-time high: By mid-2010, one in six Americans were receiving aid from antipoverty programs.[7]* For the first time since the Great Depression, Americans took more in government benefits—in the form of unemployment compensation, welfare, and other aids—than they collectively paid in taxes. Government transfer payments swelled to more than $2 trillion, more than the total amount of taxes paid by individual Americans. Not counting government employees, 64.3 million Americans depend on government to pay for food, health, and housing (up from 21.7 million in 1962). The Heritage Foundation's William Beach and Patrick Tyrell note that someone on government assistance now gets on average more than four times as much taxpayer money

---

* More than 50 million were on Medicaid (another 16 million will be added under Obamacare); more than 40 million on food stamps; 10 million on unemployment; and 4.4 million on welfare. Reported *USA Today*: "The federal price tag for Medicaid has jumped 36% in two years, to $273 billion. Jobless benefits have soared from $43 billion to $160 billion. The food stamps program has risen 80%, to $70 billion. Welfare is up 24%, to $22 billion." Even so, these numbers greatly understate the extent or cost of the dependency culture.

per year—$31,950—as he would have in 1962, adjusting for inflation.[8]* If government employees are added, more than 88 million Americans are now dependent on government for their livelihood—an increase of 163 percent since 1962.[9]

- Major Wall Street firms and failing car makers were handed hundreds of billions of dollars in taxpayer cash subsidies as rewards for their irresponsible risk taking and reckless deal making and spending. (Citigroup and General Motors each received $50 billion in direct aid; the total tab for bailouts may run into the trillions of dollars in a process that has "privatized gains and socialized losses.") Most Americans, however, were not "too big to fail" and went without bailouts.

- Middle Americans increasingly find that work no longer pays. A cover story in *Forbes* documented the perverse incentives (especially for families with college-age students) that punish success and provide incentives for lowering income.[10]

- Contemporary politics is dominated by the freebie. Cash for Clunkers: Other people buy you a car (and destroy perfectly good ones in the process). Home credits: Other people help buy you a house. Pork spending: Other people pay for your goodies. In the ultimate moocher culture, someone else buys your food, provides housing, heating, transportation, takes care of your kids, pays for your health care—and gives you a free cell phone.

- The casino-like mortgage bubble was succeeded by a massive transfer of wealth from taxpayers to bail out reckless lenders

---

* The Catalogue of Federal Domestic Assistance lists 2,025 federal subsidy programs, including 383 Health and Human Service programs, 230 in Agriculture, and 168 in Education, each with active, organized, and well-connected interest groups braying for increased funding. The result has been an explosion in the proportion of the national income paid by government rather than earned in the private sector.

and borrowers alike, adding to the nation's exploding deficit. The unaffordable was bailed out by the unsustainable.

• A law professor from the University of Arizona argues that far more of the estimated 15 million American homeowners underwater on their mortgages should stiff their lenders and walk away from their mortgages. For good measure he suggests a spending binge before defaulting.[11] As a sign that the stigma of default is fading, *The Wall Street Journal* reports that more homeowners are taking his advice and "deciding to abandon their loan obligations even if they can afford the payments."[12]

• The gap between the two Americas (the public and private sectors) continues to grow. According to the Bureau of Economic Analysis, federal employees now earn more than double what private sector workers make. In 2009, the average federal civil servant pulled down pay and benefits of more than $123,000, while private employees made do with an average of $61,051 in total compensation. The gap between the two Americas has grown in the last decade, with the gap between the compensation of federal and private workers more than doubling.[13] In addition to the cushier salaries and benefits packages, government workers on average also have more job security and far richer pensions (and more vacation days).

• The number of Americans now using food stamps has exploded even as the stigma of dependency has declined.[14] Food stamp use hit a record 42.4 million in November 2010—a 58.4 percent jump in just three years.[15] One in eight adults and one in four children now use the subsidy. One academic study found that fully half of Americans—and fully 90 percent of black children—at one time or another received food stamps before the age of 20.[16]

- Even as dependence on government rose, *USA Today* reported that income from the private sector dropped to its lowest share of American personal income in history. In the first quarter of 2010, only 41 percent of the nation's personal income came from private business paychecks. Individuals received nearly a fifth of their income from government programs.[17] Another 10 percent was paid in salaries and wages to government workers; when the cost of lavish fringe benefits is added, the proportion swells even more.

- We are extending dependency throughout society both vertically and horizontally. By legislative fiat the new health care bill extends the dependency of children to age 26, at least when it comes to health insurance, thus codifying a rolling redefinition of the age of independence. The legislation also expands the scope of middle-class dependency by providing government subsidies for health insurance to families making up to roughly $88,000 a year. By 2019, according to the Congressional Budget Office, Obamacare will add another 16 million dependents to Medicaid, while another 19 million will receive taxpayer subsidies for their health insurance. By that year, the government will be responsible for 52 percent of the nation's health care spending.[18] This guarantees that dependency will begin at birth and extend throughout the adult life of many Americans.

- The 2011 federal budget envisioned a vast, permanent expansion of the welfare state, even after the recession ends. President Obama's budget called for spending more than 10.3 trillion on poverty programs over the next ten years.[19]

- Central cities have become laboratories of mooching where the focus of political and economic activity is the expansion of or access to benefit programs, support programs, or, in the better cases, government jobs with high security and lavish benefits but little accountability. In particular, public education systems have become massive jobs programs (exemplified by the "rubber rooms" set aside for tenured teachers who can't be fired) and perfect expressions of the moocher culture: You don't expect much of me and I won't expect much of you.

• To pay for all of this, taxes on future generations will have to be more than doubled to pay off an exploding national debt, which will reach 100 percent of the Gross Domestic Product (GDP) within a decade. By 2020, nearly half of all income tax revenues will go toward paying interest on the national debt.[20] By 2050, the national debt will rise to more than 300 percent of the GDP; by 2080, it will be eight times the size of the entire economy.[21]

OPM
(Other People's Money)

This blizzard of transfer payments is advanced by advocates and politicians who rely on what William Voegeli wryly calls "non-Euclidean economics," in which taxpayers are led to believe that all of these goodies are paid for by someone else. By "blackening the skies with criss-crossing dollars," writes Voegeli, "the welfare state manages people's perceptions of its costs and benefits to encourage them to believe an impossibility; that every household can be a net importer of the wealth redistributed by the government."[22]

But despite the fondest hopes of those chasing the criss-crossing dollars, multiple mooches do not cancel each other out. The young may mooch off the old, the old off the young, but the result is not a wash. Rather, the mooching creates the habit and the expectation of relying on others; everyone feels not only entitled to the wealth of others, but convinced that they have to keep mooching or be left out. Only suckers pass up the free money.

The effect of all this on the national character goes beyond the impact on the economy. A culture of mooching undermines responsible behavior by rewarding and subsidizing failure, irresponsibility, and dependency.

In contemporary America, we now have two parallel cultures: an anachronistic culture of independence and responsibility, and the emerging moocher culture. We continually draw on the reserves of that older culture, with the unspoken assumption that it will always be there to mooch from and that responsibility and hard work are simply givens. But to sustain deadbeats, others have to pay their bills on time. Massive defaults are subsidized by the people who continue to meet their obligations to pay on time and in full. To paraphrase Margaret Thatcher, the problem with moochers is that sooner or later they run out of Other People's Money. This divide has become the flashpoint of American politics and will be for the next several decades.

A Moocher Checklist

✵ ✵ ✵

What precisely is a "moocher"? Herewith some preliminary steps toward a definition.

A moocher is:

- Someone who believes there is always a free lunch and that somebody else should pay for it.
- Someone who expects others to pay to clean up their messes.
- Someone who lays claim to something to which they are not rightfully due.
- Someone who shifts the cost of their own irresponsibility onto others who have behaved responsibly, who, as a matter of choice, takes from or relies on the efforts and resources of others.
- Someone who takes unfair advantage of others to enrich themselves or otherwise bail themselves out.
- Someone who is a recipient of the transfer of wealth created by others (without just cause) or lives off the productive efforts of others and appropriates the fruits of their enterprise without making a proportionate contribution.
- Someone who voluntarily seeks to be dependent on others.

Are you a moocher? Here is a handy checklist:

☐ Are you over 21 and living at your mother's house?

☐ Does the government send you more money than you pay in federal income taxes?

☐ Have taxpayers bought you breakfast, a car, or a house in the last few years? (Please include tax credits for clunkers, electric cars, and new home purchases.)

☐ Has the government paid you not to grow something? Have you received "disaster aid" without having suffered any losses from a disaster?

☐ Do you receive payments from pension funds that are disproportionate to your contributions?

☐ Do you routinely get something for nothing?

☐ Do you work for Goldman Sachs, Citigroup, AIG, or the government?

☐ Have you walked away from your mortgage?

☐ Do you think the government has a stash of cash that you are entitled to draw from?

☐ Are you an able-bodied, childless adult who spends his/her day playing Guitar Hero, watching *The View,* or surfing the Net while your spouse works to support you?

☐ Do you work for a lobbyist, "public affairs" company, or other corporate group whose job it is to seek privileges, benefits, or pork from government?

☐ Are you living off or depending on money that will have to be paid back by your children and grandchildren?

If you answered yes to any of the above, chances are quite good that you are a citizen of Moocher Nation.

Chapter 2

HAVE WE REACHED THE TIPPING POINT?

By 2004, the nonpartisan Tax Foundation calculated, 20 percent of U.S. households were already getting about 75 percent of their income from the federal government. Government programs accounted for at least 40 percent of the income of another 20 percent of households, meaning that two in five households were reliant on the government for their livelihoods.[1]

Roughly 60 percent of American households actually were receiving more government benefits and services than they were paying back in taxes, and the Tax Foundation estimated that under the 2009 federal budget, 70 percent of households would take in more than they contribute.

"Look at it this way," commented Rep. Paul Ryan (R-Wis.), "three out of ten American families are supporting themselves plus— through government—supplying or supplementing the incomes of seven other households. As a permanent arrangement, this is individually unfair, politically inequitable, and economically dangerous."

The numbers, said Ryan, suggest that we are approaching or perhaps have even passed a "tipping point." Once we pass that point, he says, "we will become a different people."

The Sucker Principle

The explosion of free taxpayer cash has its own seductive logic.

If the government is handing out money, the argument goes, who am I to say no? Subsidies for flood insurance for my beachfront villa? Payments to farmers for disasters they didn't suffer or for crops they never grew? Tax credits to buy myself a new car? Debit cards and free stays on luxury liners? In many circumstances the decision to pocket the free money is completely rational, if occasionally distasteful to both payers and payees. No one wants to be the first to walk away empty-handed, and everyone hopes they will be able to cash in before the pyramid collapses.

So what is the tipping point for most people?

Think about the common experience of standing in a line, for a bus, concert tickets, or a ride at Disney World. Generally, people will wait their turn, recognizing that the first-come, first-served system is, if not strictly fair, at least manageable and comprehensible and will in all likelihood result in getting on the bus, obtaining the tickets, or getting on the ride.

The queue is maintained by cultural norms and social pressure. If someone tries to jump the line, fellow line-goers likely will object and attempt to enforce the rules. But what if their attempt fails? What happens if not just one or two but dozens of individuals begin ignoring the line, jumping ahead of others and getting their hands on scarce and coveted tickets or bus seats?

Think of it as the sucker principle: The line remains intact only until those who play by the rules and wait patiently in line begin to regard themselves as suckers.

Now consider what happens when society's rewards go to those who jump the line and grab the subsidies, transfer payments, and other freebies offered by the government rather than to those who work, invest, and save prudently.

Tipping Points

One of the central questions of this book is whether we are at or nearing that "tipping point."

- When do independent, self-sufficient men or women realize that they are society's suckers, being made to work for the benefit of an ever-growing, ever-shifting, and increasingly insistent and more grasping class of moochers? When do they decide to jump the line?

- When does the principled politician who ran for office against pork and waste look around him at the rush for boodle and recognize that he and his constituents are being left out of one of history's great cash grabs? And when does he join the rush for the freebies?

- When does a businessman decide that the competitive free market—producing good products at a reasonable price—is a fool's game when competitors have invested more in clout than innovation? When does he decide that the free market is all well and good in principle but that a realist has to play the game of political grease to get access to cash subsidies, tax credits, pork barrel largesse, or mandates that compel the purchase of their product or service? When does the lobbyist become more important than the engineer, and the political fixer become more important than marketers, or designers? When do lawyers become more critical than the salesperson or the vice president of research?

Are we already there?

Plunder

In his classic *The Rise and Decline of Nations,* economist Mancur Olson describes the turning point in societies when special-interest coalitions emerge that are dedicated to seeking special privileges and benefits. Olson calls them "distributional coalitions" because they are focused not on increasing productivity or prosperity but rather on trying to "capture a larger share of the national income" through lobbying, pushing for more government regulations that protect and benefit them, while also engaging in what other economists call "rent-seeking," an inelegant term that essentially means mooching. Over time, these "distributional coalitions" cause growth to stagnate, and change the character and culture and ultimately the identity of a society.

"The incentive to produce is diminished," writes Olson, while "the incentive to seek a larger share of what is produced [by others] increases. The reward for pleasing those to whom we sell our goods and labor declines, while the reward for evading or exploiting regulations, politics, and bureaucracy and for asserting our rights, through bargaining or the complex understandings, becomes greater."[2]

"These changes in the patterns of incentives in turn deflect the direction of a society's evolutions," writes Olson, as he describes how a dynamic economy stagnates, then atrophies, and ultimately goes into decline.

Another early prophet of the rise of Moocher Nation, economist Frederic Bastiat, warned of what he called "the fatal tendency that exists in the heart of man to satisfy his wants with the least possible effort," which explains man's propensity for looting, rather than labor. Since men naturally gravitate toward the easiest path, "it follows that men will resort to plunder whenever plunder is easier than work." When that tipping point is reached, wrote Bastiat, "neither religion nor morality can stop it."

The whole point of the rule of law, argued Bastiat, was to make sure that plunder was not more rewarding than labor, and therefore its goal should always be "to protect property and punish plunder."

But Bastiat envisioned a world turned upside down: "It is impossible to introduce into society a greater change and a greater evil than this: the conversion of the law into an instrument of plunder."[3]

Celebrating Dependency

Not everyone, however, sees this "tipping point" as a bad thing; some leading "progressives" see the growth of dependency as an opportunity for political success.

Writing in *The Atlantic*, liberal analyst Thomas Edsall made a compelling case for the rise of a coalition of takers and dependents that will dominate American politics. In an article entitled "The Obama Coalition," Edsall argued that such a coalition of those dependent on government aid, public employees, minorities, unions, and other "Social Democrat"–minded liberals could cobble together a majority that would use its clout to spread around even more wealth.[4]

Edsall makes the "progressive" case for the "tipping point": More than one out of every four dollars of personal income in the United States, he notes, is now paid for with tax dollars. The percentage of Americans receiving government-financed medical coverage from Medicare or Medicaid has risen from 21 percent of the population in 1987 to 28.4 percent of the population in 2008, meaning that more than one in four were dependent on taxpayer-funded health care—even before the enactment of Obamacare.

"Over the last two years," he wrote, "there has been a massive increase in the number of people who have no place to turn except to the government." The passage of health-care legislation will accelerate the process, since a trillion dollars or so will be added to the totals of government transfer payments.

Edsall, who covered national politics for *The Washington Post* for a quarter-century, surveyed the economic and political scene and sees opportunity for the left: The Great Recession and the nation's fiscal crisis "and a demographic transition moving the nation closer to a non-white voting majority," he writes, have "revived, enlarged, and intensified the battle for limited government resources— pitting those seeking to protect what they have against those seeking more."

Constituencies "seeking more" from government are expanding, writes Edsall, noting that "three previously-marginalized groups— unmarried women, Latinos, and African Americans—made up 43 percent of the total electorate and just over 62 percent of the voters who backed Obama." (Note here Edsall's assumption that unmarried women, Latinos, and African Americans by definition support a growth in the dependency culture.)

Edsall envisions "the possibility that the political strength of voters whose convictions are perhaps best described as Social Democratic in the European sense is reaching a significant level in the United

States," and if effectively organized, "such voters are positioned to set the agenda in the Democratic Party in the near future."

Essentially, Edsall and Paul Ryan are making parallel arguments; they agree that the nation is at a tipping point. In that sense, they are both right: The battle lines of the next few decades have been drawn. But where Edsall applauds the rise of a coalition of the dependent, Ryan sees an economic and cultural disaster.

"Before the 'tipping point,' Americans remain independent and take responsibility for their own well-being," said Ryan. "Once we have gone beyond the 'tipping point,' that self-sufficient outlook will be gradually transformed into a soft despotism a lot like Europe's social welfare states. Soft despotism isn't cruel or mean, it's kindly and sympathetic. It doesn't help anyone take charge of life, but it does keep everyone in a happy state of childhood. A growing centralized bureaucracy will provide for everyone's needs, care for everyone's heath, direct everyone's career, arrange everyone's important private affairs, and work for everyone's pleasure."

The Assumption of Incompetence

Ryan, of course, is right: There is a profound difference in the mentality, morality, and politics of the independent citizen and the moocher. You cannot be a moocher without surrendering, roughly in this order: your self-respect, your independence, and ultimately your freedom. Dependency fundamentally changes the relationship between the government and the governed; even a successful supplicant is, after all, still a supplicant. By definition, dependents have to focus on and cling to their sense of victimhood/incapacity. Politically, they must also rely on the acquisition of political favoritism and influence to continue to meet their needs. Moocher Nation is incompatible with the idea of Americans as capable and independent citizens; it is, however, entirely consistent with a vision of America as a land of dysfunctional victims.

Here we come to one of the great dividing lines in debates over the future of American society: The view that encourages independence is based on having at least some confidence that individuals have the capacity to both survive and thrive if they are responsible for their own welfare and prosperity.

This includes a default setting that assumes that the average American is competent to navigate his own life; that parents are capable of raising their own children; and that given a dynamic economy, most Americans are fully able to pursue happiness with only an occasional helping hand. An example: The GI Bill was underpinned by the well-founded assumption that given a chance at a college education, the Greatest Generation would be able to take advantage of the opportunity—and it was. Similarly, in the private sector the decision to make an investment or offer a job is an act of confidence that others will be able to meet expectations and challenges. In contrast, Moocher Nation starts with the assumption that without a handout, people won't be able to cut it.

Obviously, both assumptions carry a grain of truth. Some individuals are actually quite dysfunctional and unable to thrive in families, schools, workplaces, or society. But when advocates, for example, push for the universalization of free breakfasts in schools, they are not addressing such outliers. Behind and underlining their argument is always the assumption that parents simply cannot be trusted to feed their kids.

The Assumption of Incompetence drives the expansion of both the nanny and the moocher state because rather than starting from the premise that individuals are intelligent, responsible, and capable of (fill in the blank here: caring for their kids; paying for their dinners, cell phones, or cars . . .), their default position is to assume that most Americans are unable, incapable, and incompetent—and therefore must be cared for.

All of this "caring" is compassionate, but it is also smothering. In effect, the caring class says, putting its arm tightly around the shoulder of the disadvantaged victim, "We care about you so much that we'll take over from here and run your life for you." No matter how you cut it, dependency ultimately meets loss of control. While it masquerades as compassion, the Assumption of Incompetence is an attitude that treats its objects with a mixture of pity and contempt and, therefore, not surprisingly, ends up robbing them of both self-respect and self-control. As free-market economist Friedrich Hayek understood, dependence can lead to serfdom, no matter how many euphemisms are applied to it.

Moocher's Dilemma

✽　✽　✽

Consider the escalating temptations and moral dilemmas in the following scenarios:

1. Car keys are left in the ignition of a parked car and the motor is left running. Do you take advantage of the situation and drive off in the car? Why or why not?

2. The clerk at the grocery store gives you too much money in change. Do you keep it? Do you point out the mistake? Why or why not?

3. Your bank statement includes a much larger balance than you believe is warranted. You realize the bank has made a mistake and credited your account with too much money. Do you take the money, or do you call your bank? Why or why not?

4. A government employee comes to your door with a check for disaster aid. You have done nothing to deserve the money and have suffered no damage, but he explains it is perfectly legal and you are entitled to the cash. If you object at all, he will simply point out that if you don't accept the check, it will be divided up among your neighbors, who will therefore get larger shares. Do you accept the check? Do you think most people would accept it?

Is your decision based on character, morality, or simple common sense? Or simply on the basis of what you expect your neighbor will do?

Who is responsible for this moral dilemma?

Part Two

THE JOYS OF DEPENDENCY

Chapter 3

THE RISE OF MOOCHER NATION

Calling San Francisco a laboratory for Moocher Inc. is inadequate as a description. With its bloated social service bureaucracy, massive antipoverty budgets, and smugly romantic attitudes toward the poor, San Francisco is more like a Jurassic Park for the politicized dependency culture; ideas and policies long thought extinct still roam the streets in the city by the Bay. Without San Francisco, it might be impossible to credibly describe what it was like in cities like New York in the late 1960s and early 1970s, where the modern mooching culture took root.

San Francisco has not only been conspicuously tolerant, it has been flamboyantly generous: The city has spent billions of dollars and created a vast network of indulgent social service agencies and policies for its street people. When businesses, residents, and tourists complain about dysfunctional behavior, including aggressive mooching, sleeping on sidewalks, or loitering around businesses, the city's "progressive" elites can be counted on to denounce them as racist or hard-hearted. Measures to enact even modest restrictions on the behavior of the street people are routinely opposed by the city's civil-liberties-loving, do-your-own-thing crowd.

The results have been . . . impressive.

The sidewalks in the one-time epicenter of the "Summer of Love," the Haight Ashbury district, writes Heather Mac Donald in an extraordinary bit of on-site reporting, "have been colonized by aggressive, migratory youths who travel up and down the West Coast panhandling for drug and booze money."[1] The conglomeration of interest groups and advocates and helping professions Mac Donald calls "Homelessness, Inc." insists that the panhandlers be regarded as "victims" of an uncaring society that has failed to provide sufficiently for their needs. But listen as Mac Donald describes an encounter with "four filthy targets of Homelessness, Inc.'s current relabeling effort": "[They] sprawl across the sidewalk on Haight Street, accosting pedestrians. 'Can you spare some change and shit? Will you take me home with you?' Cory, a slender, dark-haired young man from Ventura, California, cockily asks passersby, 'Dude, do you have any food?'"

This, of course, is mooching boiled down to its purest essence. The young bums have no apparent interest in obtaining housing, temporary or otherwise, and seem to have only the vaguest goals for the future. Many of them, writes Mac Donald, "see themselves as on a 'mission,' though they're hard-pressed to define it. Sometimes they follow rock bands, and other times more mysterious imperatives. . . . Some are runaways; some are college dropouts; others are years older."

All they appear to have in common, writes Mac Donald, is an "acute sense of entitlement."

"I ask the group on the blanket: Why should people give you

money? 'They got a dollar and I don't,' Cory replies. Why don't you work? 'We do work,' retorts Eeyore. 'I carry around this heavy backpack. We wake up at 7 AM and work all day. It's hard work.' She's referring to begging and drinking."

Mac Donald asks them if they aren't embarrassed to be begging. "I'm not begging," one answers. "I'm just asking for money." He is, Mac Donald writes, "seemingly convinced of the difference."

Taxpayers do their share in underwriting these lifestyles. Mac Donald encounters a "strapping young redhead trudging down Haight Street with a bedroll and a large backpack" who enthuses about the advantages of electronic food stamp cards, which allow him to access his benefits "wherever he happens to be—whether in Eugene, Oregon, where he started his freight-train route last Halloween, or in California."

These contemporary street people are practitioners of what historian Fred Siegel has called "dependent individualism," a sort of militant moocherism, in which individuals believe they are entitled to whatever lifestyle they choose, no matter how dysfunctional, "with an equally fundamental right to be supported at state expense." Siegel cites the story of one angry welfare mother who declared: "I've got six kids, and each one of them has a different daddy. It's my job to have kids, and your job, Mr. Mayor, to take care of them."[2]

Writes Siegel: "The mother was a dependent individualist. Not only was she entitled to public support, but she was entitled to that support on her own terms."[3] The dependent individual is a politically empowered moocher and they were ascendant in the late sixties.

But they can still be found in places like San Francisco, in spite of, or rather because of, the massive ongoing spending on their behalf. The city spends roughly $3 billion on social services, or more than triple the amount spent on police and fire departments. In 2009 alone, without appreciably improving the problem, the city spent $175 million on homelessness, or as Heather Mac Donald calculates, the equivalent of $26,865 in services for each of the city's 6,514 "homeless" persons.[4] For that amount of money, the city could have provided each and every street person an apartment, but advocates continue to push for more spending, blaming the condition of the homeless on the meagerness of existing housing programs. "Homelessness, at its core, is an economic issue," intones the area's Coalition on Homelessness. "People are homeless because they cannot afford rent."[5]

Nonsense, says Mac Donald: "The Haight punks may not be able to afford rent, but that is because they choose to do no work and mooch off those who do. Further, they are not *looking* for housing. They have no intention of settling down in San Francisco or anywhere else. The affordability or unaffordability of rent is thus irrelevant to their condition."

But they must be permitted to pursue their bliss . . . at someone else's expense. When city residents began pushing for a so-called Civil Sidewalks measure that would give police the right to ticket bums who are sleeping or lying down, homeless advocates denounced them as selfish bigots.* "This issue makes me sick to my stomach," said one advocate. "It makes me sick because we're putting into place another law that promotes hatred and that will codify economic profiling."[6]

This sort of rhetoric would not have been out of place in New York circa 1969, and thereby hangs a tale.

If the ideology that spawned such ideas began with a misty dream of egalitarian compassion, it ended with the squalor of Haight Ashbury and the devastated inner cities of dozens of major cities. In his

---

* Although defeated by the Board of Supervisors, the so-called sit/lie ordinance, which banned sitting or lying on public sidewalks citywide between 7 A.M. and 11 P.M., was approved by voters in November 2010.

seminal work *The Dream and the Nightmare,* Myron Magnet described the transformation of culture and policy that destroyed families, communities, and cities. Throughout the sixties, wrote Magnet, popular culture "downplayed the personal responsibility, self-control, and deferral of gratification that it takes to succeed." In place of those bourgeois values the new culture "celebrated an 'if it feels good' self-indulgence" that shaped public policy, especially for the poor. Of course, the middle classes paid a steep price for such indulgence, but when those same fashionable ideas "reached the poor, especially the urban, minority poor," wrote Magnet, "the result was disastrous."[7]

Guilt, Fear, and the Rolling Riot

So how did it happen at all?

In his history of the decline and fall of some of America's great urban centers, Fred Siegel tracks the origins of this disastrous freak show of crackpot leftism to a combination of guilt and fear. The large-scale riots of the midsixties were followed by a chronic fear of the violence Siegel calls a "rolling riot," including a dramatic spike in violent crime. For many on the left, the message was clear: "Be prepared to pay up or be prepared for trouble. In the decades that followed the 1960s, the riot ideology, a racial version of collective bargaining, became part of the warp and woof of big-city politics."

Urban leaders used fear of violence to push for more cash from the federal government "on the threat that the Casbah might again erupt." But, notes Siegel, "the most exquisite form of intimidation came in intellectual life, where cowed intellectuals relinquished their independence of judgment."[8]

In his prize-winning book *From Opportunity to Entitlement,* Gareth Davies chronicles the transformation of traditional New Deal liberalism into a doctrine of entitlement welfarism that effectively destroyed the Great Society and turned voters away from the left for years.* In a shift that alienated much of Middle America, Davies writes, "notions of self-help and personal independence . . . largely disappeared from liberal discourse during the late 1960s and 1970s. In their place came radical notions of income by right. . . ." Among activists and the liberal elite, it became common to denigrate anyone "who made demands on the poor."[9]

The sixties were not an era of subtlety or euphemism: entry-level jobs were equated with slavery; work requirements were denounced as racist; suggestions that family disintegration contributed to poverty were censured as "blaming the victim."

Liberals vied with one another to embrace the new ethos, in an orgy of what sociologist James Coleman was to call "conspicuous benevolence," designed to advertise as ostentatiously as possible their "egalitarian intentions."[10]

"Once the language of group rights and racial justice had entered antipoverty discourse," recounts Davies, "the language of mutual obligation tended to be relegated, if not abandoned altogether."[11]

Politically the idea was a disaster. Entitlement liberalism abandoned "the link between work and income at a time when the public devotion to the link was so obvious."[12] The result "left the Democratic Party astonishingly distant from the work ethic of Middle America."[13] But not before it had transformed the face of inner cities across the country and cemented notions of entitlement in at least some parts of the political culture.

---

* The subtitle of his book is *The Transformation and Decline of Great Society Liberalism.* Davies writes from a generally liberal position that largely defends FDR liberalism against the postmodern version that arose in the late 1960s.

Explosion

New York was ground zero for the accompanying explosion in welfare dependency and the attendant social collapse. In the fifteen years after the end of World War II, welfare in the city grew by just 47,000 recipients. From 1960 through 1965, it grew more rapidly, with around 200,000 clients added to the rolls, bringing the total to roughly 538,000. But then came the deluge. Under liberal mayor John Lindsay and his welfare chief, Mitchell Ginsberg (known as "Come-and-Get-It Ginsberg"), the city consciously set out to expand the welfare rolls as quickly as possible, even though the late sixties were a period of economic prosperity, and black unemployment in the city was only around 4 percent. The administration succeeded spectacularly: By 1971, New York had added another 630,000 welfare dependents, ballooning the total to more than 1,165,000. "New York's welfare population was larger than the population of fifteen states," notes Siegel. As recently as 1960, there had been 10 workers for every 1 person on the dole; by 1971 that had been cut to a ratio of just 5 to 1.[14]

As hundreds of thousands of city residents became wards, the repercussions mushroomed. Many black workers disappeared from the employment rolls, families disintegrated "amid an explosion of desertion, divorce and out-of-wedlock births," and the middle class headed for the exits. Other social changes, including the sexual revolution, contributed to family and social breakdown, but, says Siegel, "welfare was a key ingredient in the toxic brew that devastated vast sections of the city."[15]

The welfare explosion was accompanied by a transformation of attitudes as welfarists attacked root and branch the stigma associated with dependency. At the heart of this change of values was the belief that the poor were victims and they were therefore not responsible either for their condition or their behaviors. "The alibi industry had a justification for everything," writes Siegel. "The biggest and most important alibi was that the poor were so disadvantaged by their environment . . . that all responsibility for their fate was shifted to government. . . . The assumption that some individuals might be even partly responsible for their actions was, they insisted, entirely outdated."[16]

When Daniel Patrick Moynihan released his paper "The Negro Family: The Case for National Action" in 1965, it set off a firestorm of outrage among the new liberal elites. Moynihan warned that the wave of illegitimacy and family breakdowns was posing a daunting barrier to the realization of full equality for minorities. He wrote: "At the heart of the deterioration of Negro society is the deterioration of the Negro family. It is the fundamental source of weakness of the Negro community at the present time. . . . Unless this damage is repaired, all the effort to end discrimination and poverty and injustice will come to little."[17]

Today Moynihan's warning seems prophetic, but when it was released in 1965, it ran headlong into the rising tide of racial grievance and victimist ideology.

In an earlier book, *A Nation of Victims*, I recounted how the discussion of the "family question" fell under an extraordinary intellectual taboo that was to have appalling consequences for public policy. A white Boston sociologist named William Ryan led the way in claiming that any suggestion that the poor bore any responsibility for their plight was a form of "blaming the victim." For liberals like Ryan, being a victim of racism meant never having to say you're sorry or suffering the consequences of your misdeeds. Drop out of school? Refuse to work? Father illegitimate children? For Ryan, there was always someone else to blame, and he slammed any fellow liberal who did not embrace this position.[18]

The idea of the poor as victim was central to the new entitlement culture. In the new "politics of dependency," wrote welfare expert Lawrence Mead, indigents "claim a right to support based on the injuries of the past, not on anything that they contribute now. Wounds are an asset today, much as a paycheck was in progressive-era politics. One claims to be a victim, not a worker."[19]

Any attempt to change the behavior or conduct of the victim, Ryan insisted, was part of the overall pattern of victimization. Ryan shared some of his sharpest censures for wavering liberals who believed they could "revamp and revise the victim . . . they want to change his attitudes, alter his values, fill up his cultural deficits, energize his apathetic soul, cure his character defects, train him and polish and woo him from his savage ways." In other words, trying to get the poor to finish school, be responsible for their families, and get a job was part of "a dreadful war against the poor and oppressed."[20]

Waging such a war also consisted of focusing on minorities' lack of job skills and education or emphasizing "better values" or "habits of thrift and foresight." When Catherine Chilman in her book *Growing Up Poor* ventured a modest, almost apologetic defense of middle-class lifestyles as "more in harmony" with economic reality, Ryan denounced her ideas as "nefarious." Poverty, insisted Ryan, had nothing to do with character, skills, or indeed any characteristic of the poor themselves. Poverty was "most simply and clearly understood as a lack of money."

With that in mind, Ryan excoriated any program that even hinted at changing or "improving" the behavior of the downtrodden, including education programs that aimed to "make up for the deficiencies" in students' backgrounds that caused them to fail in school. When sociologist James Coleman found that family background was the single most important factor in educational success, Ryan howled with indignation, "Is this or is this not, a clear case of blaming the victim?" It was not. Rather, Coleman's study was a sober work of social research that has since become the basis for educational reform efforts throughout the country. But it clashed with Ryan's ideological worldview and indeed the era's dominant and fashionable ideologies of compassion.[21]

Welfare advocate Richard Elman declared that concern about the negative effects of dependency was a mere "bogeyman," and he insisted that no one should be made to feel shame for feeding from the welfare trough.[22] Since nonjudgmentalism was the flavor of the day, Elman found a receptive audience among urban intellectuals and activists alike. Mixed with a generous dose of racial guilt, his message was a recipe for a revolution of dependency. Stigmas against dependency, joblessness, and illegitimacy were ridiculed; the very idea of personal responsibility was derided as discriminatory.

Elman argued that Americans needed to "make dependency legitimate" so dependents could "consume with integrity." Members of the middle class, he insisted, "must dispel our own myth that we are not dependent and do not wish to become dependent. We must try to create even more agencies of dependency, and we must make it possible for all to make use of them equally."[23]

Policymakers set out to make it so. Under the leadership of New York's welfare chief Ginsberg, writes Siegel, "work—particularly entry level work—was, like fatherhood, placed in the trash can of history." Liberal leaders increasingly sneered at the idea that the poor should be steered toward gainful employment as an alternative to welfare. Activists insisted that it would be wrong to push the poor into what they called "dead end jobs."[24]

Arguing for the expansion of welfare, Paul Goodman insisted that "there are fewer jobs that can be done keeping one's honor and dignity." Elman jibed that the narrow-minded middle class wanted the poor "to go the hard route, to be . . . taxi drivers, restaurant employees . . . and factory hands."[25] These were jobs with no future, he insisted, and among the welfarist elite the idea that the poor should work came to be seen as reactionary, "the northern equivalent of the forced labor and debt bondage of the South." Instead, Elman declared, they should be entitled to dignity and income through welfare.

The cry was taken up by the emerging welfare rights movement. Declared welfare activist Beulah Sanders, "You can't force me to work! You'd better give me something better than I'm getting on welfare." Another welfare mother informed legislators that "we only want the kind of jobs that will pay $10,000 or $20,000. . . . We aren't going to do anybody's laundry or babysitting except for ourselves."[26]

Perhaps most famous among the would-be architects of the revolution were two Columbia poverty intellectuals, Richard Cloward and Frances Fox Piven, who quite explicitly and unapologetically "wanted to sever the connection between economic effort and outcome; they wanted, instead, to guarantee a high level of living as a matter of right."[27] The two argued that not nearly enough people were on welfare and they urged a full-out campaign to recruit more of the poor onto the welfare rolls. Their goal was quite explicitly to overload and bankrupt the antipoverty system, thus (they hoped) forcing a fundamental realignment of the nation's economy by guaranteeing the poor an annual income—regardless of their willingness to work.

This was not always an easy sell. Piven later lamented the reluctance of some civil rights leaders to embrace the culture of entitlement. "We met with [Urban League President] Whitney Young," Piven recalled, "and he gave us a long speech about how it was more important to get one black woman into a job as an airline stewardess than it was to get fifty poor families onto welfare."[28] Cloward and Piven and the emerging liberal orthodoxy, of course, thought just the opposite—welfare was far preferable to mere work—and they were willing to harness the "rolling riot" for their cause. They argued that the real power of the poor was "their ability to menace and riot." They called it the "politics of the poor," which included "rent strikes, crime, civic disruptions."[29]

By 1972, writes Gareth Davies, the entitlement mentality had come to dominate elite liberalism, crowding out notions of reciprocal obligation and personal responsibility as well as the idea that the poor would best be served by opening the doors of opportunity. By then, he writes, "it had become more common for liberals to define dignity as freedom from both hardship and from the stigma hitherto attached to dependency. . . . Dependency, in the old sense, was almost equated with independence in the new."[30]

Welfare reform in the 1990s came largely as a reaction to the excesses of the earlier period, and the rhetoric of entitlement is seldom voiced quite so explicitly now among the political classes. But the attitudes that shaped the embrace of the entitlement culture remain beneath the surface of much of our modern welfare state. Despite political setbacks that lay ahead, the sixties marked a dramatic shift in American culture.

Moocher Nation was born.

Chapter 4

THE JOYS OF DEPENDENCY

The converter boxes may not have been a tipping point, but they were surely a milestone in the willingness of Americans to rely on a beneficent government to provide them with all things good and beautiful, or just marginally convenient.

In 2009, the federal government spent nearly $2 billion on coupons to help consumers buy digital converter boxes for their television sets. Several years earlier, the federal government had mandated that television signals switch over from analog to digital and broadcasters spent millions of dollars warning viewers to make the necessary changes. Viewers who had cable or satellite TV were unaffected, as were those who had late-model television sets; but there were uncounted throngs who still relied on the older over-the-air sets. For them to be able to watch *Dancing with the Stars*, they would need to buy a box that would convert the signal to digital.

The problem was simple enough, but members of Congress

were so fearful that they would be blamed for the disruption and swamped by enraged constituents who were confronted with digital snow that they came up with a taxpayer-funded giveaway so that people would be able to continue to watch their favorite soap opera on their old analog television sets. Each TV owner who applied was to be given a $40 taxpayer-funded coupon to buy the converter box. The coupons did not pay the full cost of the converter boxes, but they were sweeteners, and millions of viewers grabbed for them.

Interestingly, the spending and the handout were not even especially controversial: The government was handing out free money, so who was there to object? Demand was so great that the government announced in January 2009 that its $1.34 billion coupon fund was exhausted (more than 24 million households had requested approximately 46 million coupons).[1] Not only did Congress extend the date for the transition from analog to digital, but it also provided another $490 million for the freebies as part of the massive stimulus package passed that year. By August 2009, consumers had cashed in nearly 34 million taxpayer-funded coupons (suggesting that millions of the free coupons went unused).

In other words, tens of millions of American tapped in to the federal treasury to pay for something that most of them could have easily afforded to pay for on their own. Millions more were lining up for Cash for Clunkers credits, weatherization credits, and subsidies for new home purchases. But it was only later that anyone seemed to wonder: How had we gotten to the point where Americans thought it was the responsibility of the government to pay for their TVs?

"If the Government Wants to Give Me Money . . ."

Less squeamish than their American counterparts, the British media routinely publishes exposés of that country's entrenched entitlement culture. What makes the accounts striking is not merely the extent and cost of the welfare state, but also the unapologetic attitudes the system of dependency has engendered among the moocher class. The *Daily Mail*, for example, profiled the upstanding Davey family, whose £815-a-week handout (roughly $1,270 U.S.*) pays for a four-bedroom house, top-of-the-line modern conveniences, and two vehicles, including a Mercedes van.[2] Courtesy of the government, the family also enjoys a forty-two-inch flat-screen television, a Wii games console, Nintendos, a computer, and four cell phones.

So generous are the benefits that Peter, the paterfamilias of the family of nine, quit work because he figured he could make more on the dole. And was he grateful for the generosity of the working taxpayers who made his lifestyle so bountiful and easy? Hardly.

Even with an annual income equivalent to $66,587 (U.S.), the couple, reported the *Mail*, still were not happy. With child number eight on the way, they demanded that taxpayers provide them a larger house. Unapologetically.

"It doesn't bother me that taxpayers are paying for me to have a large family," explained Mrs. Davey. "We couldn't afford to care for our children without benefits, but as long as they have everything

---

* Here's how it works: The Daveys receive £439 in "income support," an £87 housing benefit, £53 for "carer's allowance," £119 for "disability living allowance," £99 in child benefit, and £18 for "council tax benefit," for a total of £815 a week.

they need, I don't think I'm selfish." She added: "I don't feel bad about being subsidized by people who are working. I'm just working with the system that's there. If the government wants to give me money, I'm happy to take it. We get what we're entitled to. I don't put in anything because I don't pay taxes, but if I could work I would."

Despite filing for bankruptcy just eighteen months earlier after running up £20,000 of debt on mail-order catalogs, the couple routinely spends £2,000 ($3,170) on Christmas gifts alone. And why not? It is not, after all, their own money.

Although this is a tale from across the Atlantic, it provides a useful glimpse of what a successful product of the entitlement culture looks like. And indeed, it is hard to imagine a purer expression of the dependency lifestyle than the Daveys, who live the good life courtesy of Other People's Money without any sense of embarrassment or shame, their self-respect so firmly intact that they are looking for ways to expand their dependency, especially since the government appears so willing to continue to give them money.

There is an inevitability about all of this, since dependency tends to beget dependency rather than either self-reliance or gratitude. Even if the rather bald-faced cadging of the Davey family might be embarrassing to the original advocates of the welfare programs, the family illustrates how the war against the stigma of dependency can bear impressive fruit.

Yearning for the Dole

The same is true on this side of the pond, and the yearning for the dole is not confined to the poor. An article on *The Huffington Post* advises would-be writers to embrace their inner moocher: "Find ways to be unemployed, doing nothing, finding enough time on your hands, after you've met your basic needs, to wander into unknown realms of thought and imagination. You can't do it when you're busy working like everyone else . . . Avoid this gentle poison by figuring out *ways you can mock the system by taking from it what it needs to give you to maintain your writing, and give it nothing back in return.*"[3]* (Emphasis added.)

In other words, if not Mom or Dad or the trust fund, find someone else to cadge off of while you think about writing something.

Gratitude need not be part of the plan.

When a Boston television station, WBZ, interviewed President Obama's aunt, Zeituni Onyango, the reporter seemed taken aback at her unapologetic sense of entitlement. Despite being an illegal immigrant at the time, Aunt Zeituni had been receiving disability checks of up to $700 a month while living in taxpayer-subsidized public housing. She explained: "I didn't ask for it. They gave it to me. Ask your system. I didn't create it or vote for it. Go and ask your system."[4] And, indeed, if the government is handing out money, why not? When WBZ asked Aunt Zeituni whether, considering all that she has been given, she owes this country anything, she "said flatly that she owes this country nothing in return."

"But it's given you so much?" the reporter asked. She responded: "So? It's a free country under God."

The Problem of Poverty

The problem of poverty is that poor people in America have so much stuff.

---

* Some readers think he is merely describing graduate school. I will leave it to readers to decide if the writer was being satirical or was in earnest; in either case, his advice seems to be widely embraced.

According to Census Bureau data, 91 percent of poor households have color TVs; 89 percent have microwave ovens; 98 percent have a video recorder or DVD player; nearly two out of three have cable or satellite television; nearly a quarter have big-screen TVs; 72 percent own a car or truck; almost a third own two or more cars; 47 percent have dishwashers; more than a third have personal computers. According to census data, 43 percent of "poor" households actually own their own homes, and the average home is a three-bedroom house with one and a half baths, a garage, and a porch or patio.[5]

As analyst Robert Rector notes: "The average poor American has more living space than the average individual living in Paris, London, Vienna, Athens, and other cities throughout Europe."

To put this in even more perspective: 80 percent of poor households have air conditioning, a convenience enjoyed by just 36 percent of Americans as recently as 1970.

This doesn't mean that there is not genuine deprivation and need, but it does mean that the definition of "poor" is elastic and occasionally counterintuitive. Notes Rector: "The typical American defined as 'poor' by the government . . . is able to obtain medical care. His home is in good repair and is not overcrowded. By his own report, his family is not hungry and he had sufficient funds in the past year to meet his family's essential needs. While this individual's life is not opulent, it is equally far from the popular images of dire poverty conveyed by the press, liberal activists, and politicians."[6]

As Thomas Sowell writes, "Most people defined as poor had possessions once considered part of the middle class lifestyle. . . . Yet the rhetoric of the 'haves' and the 'have nots' continues, even in a society where it might be more accurate to refer to the 'haves' and the 'have lots.'"[7]

So what exactly constitutes being poor? At any given time the statistics are a snapshot that label as "poor" groups that may be merely passing through periods of low income, like medical students, individuals who graduate midyear and only have a partial year's income, children of the affluent who may be living with Mom and Dad, wives of rich men who earn no income, and retirees who may have considerable assets.* As Sowell notes, the official poverty statistics do not distinguish between "people whose current incomes are low and people who are genuinely poor in the sense that they are an enduring class of people whose standards of living will remain low for many years or even for life. . . ."[8] Within a year, a remarkable 40 percent of the "poor" at any given time no longer meet the criteria.

One notable incongruity in the definitions: The "poor" spend roughly $1.75 for every dollar they get in income. The paradox is easily explained: Most poverty statistics *leave out* all of the transfer payments the poor receive from various government programs, ranging from subsidized housing to food stamps. Since the lowest fifth of earners receive more than three quarters of their income from transfer payments and in-kind transfers, this omission significantly distorts the picture of poverty. Sowell notes that in 2001 such payments and transfers constituted 77.8 percent of the economic resources of the bottom fifth of earners. "In other words," he concludes, "the alarming statistics on their income so often cited in the media and by politicians *count only 22 percent of the actual economic resources at their disposal.*"[9] (Emphasis in original.)

---

* Notes Sowell: 80 percent of individuals 65 and older are either homeowners or home buyers, and those individuals report median monthly housing costs of just $339. In addition, households headed by people aged 70–74 "have the highest average wealth of any age bracket in American society" even though their income is lower. The average income of households headed by someone over the age of 65, he notes, "is nearly 3 times the wealth of households headed by people in the 35 to 44 year old bracket—and more than 15 times the wealth of households headed by people under 35 years of age." (Sowell, *Economic Facts and Fallacies*, p. 13.)

Call Me

The free cell phones are a good example. Fifty-two-year-old Leon Simmons and his wife make only about $1,600 a month after taxes. Out of that, they are able to pay $159 a month for a landline telephone, high-speed Internet access, and cable television.

But under a new program of "wireless welfare," they get their cell phone for free, complete with caller ID, call waiting, and voice mail. In a story on the rapid growth of the program, Simmons told *The New York Times* that he thought people walking around talking on cell phones look "silly." But, he says, he'll use his new one, and why not?

"It's free," he explained. And indeed it is, along with government-backed free text messaging.[10]

Low-income residents in a number of states are eligible to get free phones with limited minutes as long as they qualify for programs like Medicaid, food stamps, housing assistance, or other welfare programs and have an income up to 135 percent of the poverty level.*

Few programs illustrate the "mission creep" of antipoverty programs as clearly as the phone program, or reveal how far many of those programs have drifted from their original focus on providing basic needs to the destitute. Medicaid for the sick, shelter for the

---

* The cell phone freebies are subsidized by the Universal Service Fee, essentially a tax on phone service that was originally used to subsidize rural phone bills. The program was expanded in the Reagan years with the creation of the Lifeline program, which provided modest subsidies for the phone bills of poor people. In 1996, Congress further expanded the subsidy program by creating the Universal Service Administrative Company with the express mission of ensuring "all Americans, including low-income consumers and those who live in rural, insular, high cost areas, shall have affordable service and [to] help to connect eligible schools, libraries, and rural health care providers to the global telecommunications network." While this subsidy was largely still limited to landline phones, in 2008, under the Bush administration, it spawned a further subsidy known as Safelink, which began providing free cell phones.

homeless, food for the starving . . . cell phones for the unconnected? How far we've come. (A 2010 study by the Centers for Disease Control and Prevention found that 73 percent of adults listed as living in poverty nonetheless now own cell phones.)[11]

Most of those phones are distributed through a Mexican-owned company called TracFone. Since November 2008, the number of customers receiving free or subsidized wireless service has more than doubled to 1.4 million.

Advocates have quickly turned the perk into an entitlement. The spokesman for the leading company offering the subsidized phone says, "Having a telephone service, just in general, is not a privilege, it should be a right of each one."[12]* Presumably this means that they are entitled to free text messages, call waiting, and caller ID as well.

Always More

This relative prosperity of America's poor does not, however, slacken the drive to expand the welfare state or the left's insistence that we must do more to spread the wealth to the underprivileged.

Since the War on Poverty began, taxpayers have spent $15.9 trillion on various forms of mean-tested welfare, but the push for more continues unabated.[13] With only brief and temporary pauses, spending on welfare programs has continued to rise inexorably;

---

* Even so, TracFone apparently wants to have it both ways. In Web ads pushing the free phones to poor people in Wisconsin, for example, TracFone touts: "FREE government supported cell phone." But in a Lifeline/Safelink Fact Sheet, the company insists that "Safelink phones are not paid for by taxpayers or the federal government." This is a quibble without a distinction, since the funds are paid for from the federally created Universal Service Administrative Company, which was created by Congress, set up by the Federal Communication Commission, and funded by the Universal Service Fee, which is a tax in all but name.

antipoverty programs grow and metastasize in both times of recession and prosperity. Historian Fred Siegel notes that the welfare explosion of the 1960s "coincided with the great economic and jobs boom of the 1960s when black unemployment in the city [New York] was running at 4 percent, about half the national average for minorities."[14]

Adjusted for inflation, we now spend thirteen times as much on welfare as we did when Lyndon Johnson launched the poverty war. Not even Ronald Reagan or two subsequent Republican presidents could slow the march toward dependency. By 2007, per capita welfare spending was 77 percent higher than it was when Reagan was sworn in to office in 1981.[15] Between 1989 and 2008, welfare spending rose by a staggering 292 percent, faster than the growth of spending on Social Security, Medicare, and education, and more than twice as fast as spending on defense, despite the fact that the period included two major wars.[16]

In the next few years, even after the economic recovery, it will get much worse.

Although much of the increased spending on programs for the poor and the unemployed can be attributed to the economic downturn that began in 2007, President Obama's 2011 budget would increase welfare spending by 42 percent over 2008 spending levels, bringing spending on the poor to nearly $1 trillion a year.* This is not a temporary, stopgap, or safety net measure: The budget projects a dramatic and permanent expansion of the welfare state, even as millions of baby boomers move toward retirement.[17]

Some distinctions need to be made here: Nearly half of means-tested welfare payments go to low-income elderly in nursing homes

---

* Spending on welfare and low-income health care assistance rose 113.8 percent from 1989 to 1996, and then rose another 80.2 percent from 1997 to 2005. In just three years, from 2006 to 2009, it rose by another 43.3 percent. ("Confronting the Unsustainable Growth of Welfare Entitlements," Heritage Foundation; Office of Management and Budget, Historical Tables; Budgets of the United States.)

or to the disabled. These payments are not controversial and do not fall under the rubric of "mooching."

But the other half of welfare payments go to able-bodied adults and their children.[18] While some are undeniably poor through no fault of their own, many of the adults are poor as a result of both circumstances and their own choices, including spotty education and employment histories; many children are in poverty because they were born out of wedlock, which in turn triggers another round of dependency. As the Heritage Foundation notes: "Welfare entitlements generally begin at a child's birth. Some 40 percent of all births in the U.S. are now paid for by the Medicaid program. Most of these Medicaid-funded births occur to never-married women with low education levels. Once the taxpayer has paid for the childbirth, aid to the mother and child will generally continue through a wide variety of programs for years to come."[19]

Unfortunately, the culture of dependency perpetuates the behaviors and patterns that created the conditions of poverty in the first place, including out-of-wedlock births, which have continued to grow along with the welfare state.* In central cities, the collapse of intact families has become endemic, but nationally the illegitimacy rate for the entire population is about where the rate was in poor central city neighborhoods fifty years ago; 40 percent of births nationwide are now to single parents. And despite years of welfare "reform," relatively little is required of recipients. Most aid takes the form of "unconditional welfare assistance" for which "the recipient is required to do little or nothing in exchange for the aid," note analysts Kiki Bradley and Robert Rector. "In particular, the potential recipient is never expected to take reasonable steps to avoid future dependence."[20]

---

* "Single mothers increase their chances of living in poverty 416 percent relative to married couples. High school dropouts increase their chances of living in poverty 529 percent relative to college graduates. Not working increases the chances of living in poverty 741 percent relative to those who are working full-time." (Norman R. Cloutier, director, University of Wisconsin Parkside Center for Economic Education, December 3, 2010.)

Rather than representing a temporary hand up, the evidence also suggests that programs like food stamps, unemployment insurance, and public housing foster long-term dependency, which can be passed from generation to generation. For instance, with public housing programs, there are no time limits or work requirements. No need to get a job or move on with your life. A study of government housing programs by the Department of Housing and Urban Development in 2007 found that significant numbers of participants in public housing remained in the programs for ten years or longer.

The result is that for millions of Americans, dependency as a way of life means that their dreams and plans for the future are focused not on themselves or their own efforts or the growth of the national economy, but rather on their continuing access to Other People's Money, even if those other people are running out of it.

"Relative Deprivation"

This point needs to be made again: The expansion of dependency is no longer about ending hunger or malnutrition, or making sure the homeless have shelter, or even providing an economic safety net for the truly unfortunate. Much of that has already been taken care of. With urgent needs already met, advocates need something else to drive the expansion of the dependency state. Their latest gambit appears to be the idea of "relative deprivation."

Writing in *The New Yorker*, John Cassidy implicitly acknowledges the awkwardness of a situation in which so many of the poor have the accoutrements of middle-class life, such as color televisions and dishwashers. This, of course, does not meet any accepted definition of "deprivation," and it doesn't accord well with traditional understandings of impoverishment. It is, for example, difficult to imagine Charles Dickens's Little Nell being quite as poignant a symbol of privation if she had cable television and central air.

Similarly, it's problematic to push for continued expansion of the welfare state when the American poor are so relatively affluent. Cassidy argues that the problem is that while the poor have lots of stuff, they live in a world in which *other people have even more stuff.* The poor, he writes, "live in a society in which many families also possess DVD players, cell phones, desktop computers, broadband Internet connections, powerful game consoles, SUVs, health club memberships, and vacation homes." In other words, they may not be starving or freezing, but they are deprived in comparison to their prosperous fellow citizens. This "relative deprivation," insists Cassidy, "may limit a person's capacity for social achievement."[21]

This is "chasing your own tail" with a vengeance: If you have one car and your neighbor has two cars, you are relatively deprived. If you can afford to eat steak two nights a week, you are relatively deprived if others can dine on it three nights a week. It is not a sign of prosperity to have a Nintendo if the kid down the block has a PlayStation as well. You are both relatively deprived if another neighbor has an Xbox 360 and an iPad.

The variations are endless: The poor sap with only one house is deprived relative to the family with two houses, who are in turn relatively deprived in relation to those who might have three. I have a forty-two-inch HD television; my coworker has a fifty-two-inch plasma beauty. This pains me, but I am not sure how this is now society's problem or its obligation to fix.

Philosopher David Schmidtz is sharply critical of the new standard. "Critics of capitalism once scoffed at the clichéd suburban goal of 'keeping up with the Joneses.' Critics now treat evidence that some group is failing to get ahead of the Joneses as a basis for deeming capitalism a failure." The shift in emphasis, says Schmidtz bluntly, is "embarrassing."

"The old critique of capitalism was thoughtful," argues Schmidtz. "It was right to scoff at the goal of keeping up with the Joneses. Elevating that goal to the status of a principle of justice is mindless."[22]

By definition, the Joneses cannot be kept up with. Short of mandatory equality—everybody gets the same stuff and nobody gets anything more—there will always be the haves and have mores. But it is precisely this insolubility that makes the idea of "relative deprivation" so attractive. As a solution to the problem of actual poverty, it is hopeless, but as a rationale for the endless expansion of the welfare state, it is quite helpful.

The dependency culture needs victims, even if that victim has high-speed Internet.

The Kindness of Strangers

(A Moocher Manifesto)

✳ ✳ ✳

Addiction to digital freebies has not been limited to free cell phones or converter boxes. In a widely read op-ed column in *The New York Times*, a Brooklyn College professor, Helen Rubinstein, laments her loss of "free" Internet access.

"For a long time," she writes, "I relied on my Brooklyn neighbors' generosity—that is, their unsecured wireless networks—every time I connected to the Web."[1]

Although she teaches writing in her college classes, her use of the word "generosity" is a rather obvious misnomer: generosity implies a voluntary exchange. If her neighbors had given her permission to use their networks, it could well have been an act of generosity, but in Rubinstein's case, she was poaching their signals without their knowledge or consent. Even so, Rubinstein was unapologetic.

"It may have been unfair, but I don't believe I was stealing: the owners' leaving their networks password-free was essentially a gift, an ethereal gesture of kindness. Sometimes I'd imagine my anonymous benefactors . . . thinking, 'Well, I have Internet to spare.'"

This is a rationalization bordering on absurdism: There was no "gift," no act of ethereal "kindness," no selfless act of sharing.

Rubinstein wanted the free Wi-Fi, found it more convenient to mooch than to pay for it, and somehow transformed the freebie into a high-minded entitlement. There is no indication in her apologia that the Wi-Fi was unaffordable or that she was unable to pay for it: She simply did not *want* to pay for it.*

After she lost her signal, she writes, she debated whether she would actually pay for Internet access herself. Writing out her own check "seemed wasteful: paying a company to come wire my apartment, then paying a monthly fee so that I could maintain my own private territory within the cloud of 20 or so wireless networks that were already humming around my apartment." It would have been so much better, she suggests, if she could just pay a "nominal fee" so she could "partake of the riches that were all around me in abundance."

Rationalizing her reluctance, Rubinstein reasons that paying for Internet access "isn't like paying for cable TV, where cable providers pay cable networks in turn. . . . Nor is it like paying for phone service." After all, she writes, her e-mail address was portable, unconnected to any single computer, and completely free.

"Which is part of why getting online free felt so natural," she explains.

Rubinstein was either unaware of, or, more likely, indifferent to the

---

* The Web site for Time Warner Cable, which provides cable access in New York, explained: "WiFi theft occurs when someone installs a wireless network in a residence or business location and intentionally enables others to receive broadband service for free over their wireless network." The company cites federal law: "No person shall intercept or receive or assist in intercepting or receiving any communications service offered over a cable system, unless specifically authorized to do so by a cable operator." Violators of this statute face fines of up to $50,000 and imprisonment for up to two years on a first offense. A second offense can carry a fine of $100,000 or five years in jail. (www.timewarnercable.com/nynj/support/cabletheft/)

fact that her "free" Wi-Fi was the product of billions of dollars of investments in infrastructure that made her Internet access seem like magic or like an abundant natural resource that was there for the taking. In reality, somebody else invested in that infrastructure, took the risk, planned it, built it, while others (her neighbors) paid for it. Speaking for moochers everywhere, Rubinstein resented having to pay for conveniences others have created and maintained.

"In an ideal world," she writes, "the Internet would be universally available to anyone able to receive it." Of course in an ideal world, electricity, water, maybe even Bluetooth would be gratis; but in the real world, somebody else always has to pay.

Chapter 5

ADDICTED TO OPM (OTHER PEOPLE'S MONEY)

Free money is, naturally enough, a magnet. But it is also addictive, as the experience of forty years of welfare dependency ought to have made clear. Under the right circumstance, even genuine need morphs into mooching, complete with waste, fraud, and an unshakable and ingrained unwillingness to take personal responsibility, a phenomenon seen in microcosm in the aftermath of Hurricane Katrina, a natural disaster of biblical proportions that victimized hundreds of thousands of Gulf Coast residents. Many of them lost their homes and their livelihoods through no fault of their own.

There is no gainsaying the amount of suffering, poverty, and genuine urgency caused by the hurricane and the flooding. But it is one thing for a genuine victim to be knocked down and quite another to be playing that same card years later. What began as an outpouring of generosity and commitment to help the victims of

Katrina turned into what *The New York Times* described as "one of the most extraordinary displays of scams, schemes and stupefying bureaucratic bungles in modern history, costing taxpayers up to $2 billion."[1]

The *Times* noted that there were worse cases of government waste and fraud in history, including the 2001 discovery of as much as $12 billion in bogus Medicare benefit payments and the 2005 revelation that the Earned Income Tax Credit program had paid out $9 billion in unjustified claims (more about that later). But what the Great Katrina Rip-off lacked in dollar amounts, it more than made up for in dazzling details.

The U.S. Government Accountability Office (GAO) has estimated that more than one out of every five dollars given to "victims" of Katrina might have been improperly distributed. Post-Katrina stories of waste and fraud are legion: the $10 million paid out to more than a thousand prison inmates for "rental and disaster-relief assistance"; the half billion dollars worth of mobile homes that sat empty because of bureaucratic incompetence; the fiasco of the $2,000 debit cards that were used to buy diamond engagement rings, pornographic movies, football tickets, Caribbean cruises, a $450 tattoo, bottles of champagne at Hooters, and even $300 worth of *Girls Gone Wild* videos. The debit cards were used to make bail, pay outstanding parking fines, buy a sex change operation, and retain a divorce lawyer. Not surprisingly, many of the debit cards were issued to applicants using duplicate or invalid Social Security numbers, false addresses, and fictitious names.[2]

A program to provide free hotel rooms run by the Red Cross and paid for by FEMA resulted in what investigators later called "extraordinary abuse and waste." With good intentions exceeding caution or even basic prudence, the Red Cross didn't bother to keep track of hundreds of thousands of recipients. The GAO later found that because they asked only for zip codes—and no other documentation—the government cut rental assistance checks to people who were also getting free hotel rooms.[3]

Still, this only scratched the surface. Evacuees were put up in $438-per-night hotel rooms in New York and $375-per-night condos in Panama City, Florida, courtesy of the taxpayer. When the bills came due, taxpayers shelled out more than $62 million for hotel rooms at an average cost of $2,400 a month. Critics pointed out that this was at least three times what a two-bedroom apartment would have cost. Even this paled next to the $249 million paid out for 8,136 cruise-ship cabins to house hurricane victims for six months. Department of Homeland Security inspector general Richard L. Skinner estimated the cost of the luxury cabins to taxpayers at $5,100 a month per passenger.[4]

The tsunami of free cash also turned the heads of government employees, who did not pass up the opportunity to snag some of the bulging stash of OPM for themselves. Before officials realized this was a colossally bad idea, bureaucrats had run up millions of dollars of charges, including $150,000 worth of Jockey underwear. In most cases the government employees paid retail, apparently unaware of the concept of buying in bulk or wholesale, as most consumers using their own money would have done.[5]

Louisiana governor Kathleen Blanco also chose the occasion to spend $564,000 to remodel her staff's office. As Citizens Against Government Waste reported: "The newly refurbished office space on the sixth floor of the State Capitol includes hookups and mounts for two flat screen televisions, Swedish granite countertops, walnut paneling and frosted laminated glass. The floor, which will not be accessible to the public, was redesigned to add three new offices, a conference room and file storage areas."[6]

Learned Helplessness

But this is not a book about waste or fraud or even greedy politicians. It is about mooching; and the aftermath of Katrina is relevant here primarily as a microcosm of the addictive power of dependency, which is manifested in the learned helplessness of dependency.

"Learned helplessness" is a psychological term that describes someone who gives up striving because their actions have no effect on their environment or because they have been led to believe they have no control over circumstances or events. The term, developed by psychologist Martin Seligman, applies to both animals and humans who learn that effort is futile and therefore behave in a passive or helpless manner.

But the same concept can be borrowed to describe the sense of futility engendered by the dependency culture. The Assumption of Incompetence that pervades the welfare culture leads ineluctably to the Learned Helplessness of Dependency.

When victims are responsible for nothing, then nothing they can do will appreciably change or improve their lives. That is up to someone else, someone who pays for their housing, food, and transportation, and to whom they look to solve their problems and plan for their future. The tragedy of the cycle of poverty is that it passes this helplessness of dependency from generation to generation.

In the face of adversity, people accustomed to the lack of responsibility or independence are unlikely to respond either by taking control of the situation or by taking the initiative to extricate themselves or others from it. More likely, they will wait on others to act.

This, of course, was a scene repeated again and again in the wake of Hurricane Katrina. Along with bureaucratic incompetence and political ineptness, the aftermath of the disaster also exposed the soft underbelly of the learned helplessness begotten by decades of dependency.

After All These Years . . .

Katrina hit the Gulf Coast on August 29, 2005; but nearly a year and a half later, *The New York Times* was reporting that "life is still precarious and unpredictable for many evacuees, especially those who have depended on the government for a modicum of stability." A key measure of that dependency: More than seventeen months after the disaster, 102,000 families were still living in FEMA trailers and "an additional 33,000 [were] living in apartments paid for by FEMA."[7]

Throughout 2006 and beyond, there were stories of Katrina evacuees who had settled into their subsidized digs, reluctant to make any move. In May 2006, *New York* magazine profiled "victim" Theon Johnson, who had spent the winter after Katrina as a guest of the federal taxpayer at the JFK Holiday Inn in New York. As the magazine noted, most evacuees had gotten on with their lives, but because of the city's generous "squatters law," a judge's order was required to evict the remaining evacuees like Johnson.[8]

Johnson, forty-nine, had settled easily into his dependency. According to the account, he was usually up all night, but occasionally he would go outside and beg for change. "When Johnson's caseworker, Sharon, comes around," the magazine reported, "she gives him some bus passes and maybe a few bucks, but she's getting frustrated. 'They sit around on their butts watching TV. There's only but so much I can do if they're not willing to help themselves.'"

Johnson was given $9,000 in housing aid by FEMA, but "he spent it all on booze, cigarettes, some clothes, and food—partying, mostly." So, naturally, he waited around for the government to give him more. "I spent my money just the way I wanted, and I think [FEMA] should send me some more," he told the magazine. But that trough was closed to Johnson. His FEMA caseworkers offered to buy him a free ticket home to New Orleans, but he turned it down, instead choosing to wait until the Holiday Inn offered him a "buyout" deal, which he was hoping would be about $1,200.

A few months earlier, self-appointed "representatives of Hurricane Katrina evacuees" holed up in New York hotels demanded that the hotel's management pay families $2,500 in return for leaving.[9] What began as a public service had morphed into a shakedown that took various forms over the next few years.

In mid-2010, the Associated Press profiled residents of state-owned cottages who complained they were under pressure to move out of the free homes they had lived in since Katrina left them homeless—five years earlier. Even half a decade after the disaster, taxpayers were still paying for eight hundred state-owned cottages, in addition to two hundred federally supplied FEMA trailers.

One resident, Pete Yarborough, had spent years living in a four-hundred-square-foot cottage that sat on cinder blocks, but he was one of the squatters who refused to buy the tiny homes for as little as $351 and move them to higher ground.[10]

In fairness, Yarborough said he was put out of work by the BP oil spill in mid-2010 and complained that he was having a hard time paying his car, light, and phone bills. "Everything," he explained, "is past due." This, of course, was meant to induce sympathy. But it is worth asking: Was he unemployed for the entire five years since Katrina? According to the story, he had been hauling seafood until the BP spill, which suggests he was gainfully employed while living in the free cottage and that he stayed in the cottage as a matter of choice rather than move on with his life. And why not? For five years he lived rent free with no incentive for him to seek out better accommodations that would have required him to contribute. Far easier to stay put.

Liberal critics were quick to see the Katrina disaster as an indictment of the gap between haves and have nots and a black mark on small-government conservatism. Intoned the late senator Edward Kennedy: "What the American people have seen is this incredible disparity in which those people who had cars and money got out, and those people who were impoverished died."

But isn't it more appropriate to see Katrina as the fallout from a culture that had for decades encouraged dependency, while failing to eradicate poverty? Despite billions of dollars spent on antipoverty programs, a quarter of New Orleans residents lived in poverty, many of them in public housing even before the disaster. Dependency was already a way of life long before Katrina. As *The Wall Street Journal*'s Brendan Miniter said in the days after the flood: "These are the people who were left behind in the flood and who have long been left behind by failing schools, lack of economic opportunity, and crime well above the national average."[11] Those who could do so on their own had gotten away before the flooding. But, Miniter wrote, "those who depended on the government (and public transportation) were left for days to the mercy of armed thugs at the Superdome and Convention Center."

Even as the political class was rushing to assemble new programs, Miniter saw the disaster as a symbol of the welfare state: "Use the promise of food, shelter and other necessities to lure most of the poor to a few central points and then leave them stranded and nearly helpless."

Many of them were still stranded five years later.

Want → Need → Right

✻ ✻ ✻

(Suitable for laminating and keeping in your wallet.)

While the principle applies equally to housing, health care, cell phones, new windows, child care, and hybrids, the explosion of subsidized eats perhaps best illustrates the transformation of wants into needs and then into obligations in a moocher society.

Here's how it works:

I want you to buy me lunch.

Therefore, I need lunch.

If I need something, I have a right to it.

You therefore have an obligation to pay for my lunch, food stamps, and free tater tots for my kid.

All of these steps can be simplified thus:

Want → need → right → obligation
(food stamps, mortgage bailout, health care, free cell phones, etc.)

I can also convince you that you also have a right to lunch, and we can join together to make someone else pay to feed us, preferably someone who is 1) unpopular, 2) far away, 3) not yet born.

My appeal is also enhanced if I can insert a claim of victimization in my bid for sympathy and free hamburgers. Victims are, by definition, innocent, while their status of victimization also implies guilt on the part of others. It works this way:

Want → victim card (innocent and not responsible) → need → entitled as a matter of right → your guilt → obligation to pay → freebie

Chapter 6

FEED ME

We start them young and at the breakfast table. So many children now eat on the public dime, either at school or through food stamps, that dependence on government for food has become as much a rite of passage as puberty or acne. The habit of dependency is inculcated early.

In a move described as "locally unprecedented" by *The Philadelphia Inquirer,* that city's school district announced that henceforth the number of children eating breakfast at school would be a factor in evaluating the job performance of principals.[1] No longer would principals be judged solely on the basis of reading and math scores, disciplinary control, graduation rates, or even budget management—they now also must ensure that as many children as possible eat free breakfasts at school rather than at home.

Few forms of dependency have been pushed as aggressively or

celebrated as enthusiastically as the free meal, especially in schools, where states and districts across the country have embarked on a free-food-for-all campaign.

In Pueblo, Colorado, for instance, the schools offer free breakfast to every child regardless of need or family income "so no one is embarrassed to be eating it." *USA Today* celebrated the rise of the universal freebie in a story headlined: "Breakfast in Class: Fight Against Kids' Hunger Starts at School."[2] *Noto bene:* According to the newspaper, the fight against hunger doesn't start at home with mothers and fathers, or even with children who can pour their own bowls of cereal or butter their own toast . . . but at school. "Like it or not," reported *USA Today*, "making sure children get fed has become central to schools' mission."

So zealous are the Pueblo schools to push the taxpayer-funded breakfasts that at Centennial High School Cocoa Puffs, Lucky Charms, doughnuts, burritos, and juice are served in classrooms, thus eliminating any possible inconvenience along with the stigma. The push is already on in schools across the country to emulate the eat-at-school programs, paid for by federal taxpayers. Not surprisingly, a 2001 pilot program at seventy-nine schools found that offering free breakfast to every child actually increased participation; serving it in class boosted participation to 65 percent. Explained *USA Today*: "Feeding free breakfast to students who can afford to pay avoids the stigma for students who can't but don't want everyone to know. Serving breakfast in class means kids don't have to get there early to be fed. . . . Bus schedules, parents' work schedules, and, for high school students, *the desire to sleep as late as possible make getting to school early for breakfast difficult.*"[3] (Emphasis added.)

In Case You Hadn't Noticed, the Kids Are Fat

As urgent as the problem of letting teenagers sleep late may be, there are other more awkward issues with the crusade for free breakfasts: It is a dependency program in search of a problem. The push for more meals at schools comes at a time when it is increasingly obvious that the real problem with America's youth is not, in fact, their lack of food. If America's children were actually in the throes of famine or the landscape were littered with victims of deprivation, even an expensive program might be justified. In fact, however, there is scant evidence that young people are experiencing anything like an epidemic of hunger.

Indeed, the growing epidemic of childhood obesity poses a real problem for the Hunger Lobby: While the scrawny, undernourished child with large, pleading eyes is compelling, the child with multiple chins elicits a different reaction—generally not a desire to buy him a free meal. A generation of youngsters with generous posteriors requires a whole new terminology.

The Hunger Lobby's response? A new euphemism: The kids may not be hungry or even undernourished; instead, they are "food insecure."

"Food insecurity" is useful for advocates in that it is both alarming and nebulous. It is worrisome enough to inspire concern for deprived urchins, but elastic enough to cover children who are not by any reasonable measure either actually hungry or underfed— who might, in fact, be quite fat.

Lexuses and Free Breakfast

In Philadelphia, every student—all 165,000—is eligible for free, taxpayer-funded breakfasts, regardless of their income. For reasons that baffled and frustrated officials, only 54,000 students actually took advantage of the district's generosity—thus the new pressure on principals to make sure that children do not eat at home with their parents.

Pennsylvania officials, in fact, were so eager to increase participation in the free breakfasts that they declared that if students ate in their first class period, it would be counted as "instructional time," as long as a teacher was present.

Of course, Philadelphia is a high-poverty area, and advocates can claim that many of the children would otherwise go hungry if not fed by the public schools. But how to explain Mequon-Thiensville, Wisconsin?

The affluent Milwaukee suburb was named the winner of the "Wisconsin School Breakfast Challenge" by the state's Department of Public Instruction for increasing in-school breakfast participation by 110 percent over the 2007–08 school year. "A value meal option was also marketed," the state education department explained, "to attract more students to take a reimbursable meal."[4]

Mequon-Thiensville posted the largest one-year growth in in-school breakfast of any large district, despite the fact that the community had a median family income of more than $107,000 (more than twice the state and national averages). The mean value of a house in Mequon-Thiensville in 2010 was $471,353, but heaven forbid schoolchildren would partake of their morning meals at any of those homes.

Parents who routinely sign up their children for hockey, tennis, and cello lessons; provide them with smartphones, Internet access, and Xbox 360s; drive them to school in late-model Lexus SUVs; or give their 16-years-olds new cars to drive themselves—apparently cannot be expected to toss an Eggo into the toaster in the morning. On the contrary, they are actively discouraged from doing so as a matter of public policy.

The contest won by the Mequon-Thiensville schools was part of a much larger effort by the state education bureaucracy to increase school breakfasts throughout Wisconsin by 50 percent. By 2010, 1,690 schools served breakfast (still short of the 2,598 serving lunch) and state officials boasted that they served more than 125,000 school breakfasts each day—with 74 percent of the students eligible for free or reduced-price meals.

Zealous education officials even held workshops at Ramada Inns to "show attendees new ways to attract students to their breakfast programs."

"Serving breakfast in the classroom during first or second hour has proven to be extremely successful," explained one presenter. "Many schools use this model without it affecting instructional time much at all." The key word here is "much," but note also the expansion into midmorning. "A mid-morning breakfast might be especially beneficial for those students who are just not hungry when they first wake up in the morning and skip breakfast before coming to school," said one official. "Having access to a breakfast meal a bit later provides them with the morning sustenance they need to learn in school."[5]

Despite all the talk about children's nutrition, however, the workshops also focused on what really mattered: getting the cash. They included "sessions on topics such as grant writing 101, low-budget marketing strategies," and, of course, "information about maximizing reimbursement rates."

This suggests that the sudden doubling of breakfasts-in-school was clearly not a response to a sudden spike in childhood malnutrition; it was expanding the program for the sake of expanding the program and accessing the extra dollars attached to the school meals.

Like so many other government programs of its kind, the school lunch program can trace at least some of its history to the Depression era, when the Roosevelt administration put the government in the business of regulating agricultural prices in part by having it buy up huge volumes of surplus commodities and then redistributing the food. Over time, the Department of Agriculture began transferring much of the extra foodstuffs to public schools, a move popular with farming interests and their allies in Congress. One benefit of the food-for-schools programs was that farm interests could be confident that the surplus would not (a) be resold in the marketplace, or (b) replace the sales of other produce. In other words, school lunches were at least in part a form of corporate welfare for farmers, which helps to explain why the lunches were often so lousy.[6]

To this day, most commodities bought by the government and made available to schools are purchased with an eye toward regulating food markets and subsidizing farm incomes, not benefiting the waistlines of children. In 2003, for example, the feds spent a billion dollars on commodities that were eventually served up by lunch ladies. As White House chef Sam Kass noted: "Two thirds of that bought meat and dairy, with little more than one quarter going to vegetables that were mostly frozen."[7]

The developments seem to fulfill the aspirations of the legendary liberal warhorse Hubert Humphrey, who pushed for federal funding to provide every student in the country a free daily lunch. David Stockman, who was President Reagan's budget chief, noted that since the government already provided free meals to poor children, the only apparent benefit was to give more affluent families "the privilege of buying school lunches on an annual purchase plan every April 15."[8] But even Humphrey could hardly have envisioned the scope of the expansion of the feed-me state.

As William Voegeli notes in *Never Enough,* professional liberalism's "indifference to whether or not programs are effective or whether they help people who really need it" means that the default position of the welfare state is to always throw a bigger net. How big should the welfare state be? What would be enough? Writes Voegeli: "The answer to this question is . . . well, that there is no answer to this question. Liberals could tackle this problem at the macro-level, describing the boundaries beyond which the welfare state need not and should not expand. They never do."[9]

This principle is illustrated by the expansion of breakfast into midmorning on the grounds that mere breakfast is no longer sufficient and that there is never enough taxpayers can do for hungry little ones. And indeed, the push for breakfast had no sooner gone *en fuego* than the campaign to provide free *dinners* began in earnest as well. In December 2010, the lame duck Democratic Congress approved a $4.5 billion "child nutrition bill" that not only expanded the number of children eligible for subsidized lunches, but also funded a program to provide another 20 million *after-school* meals.[10] In Pueblo, Colorado, educrats have gone even further. Schools have begun sending bags of food home with children on Fridays "to get them through the weekend." Can food for summer vacation be far behind?[11]

The expansion of childhood food dependency is defended and indeed insisted upon in the name of "the children," who, advocates insist, would inevitably go hungry were it not for government aid. Wisconsin's education chief declared: "A hungry child can't learn. It is encouraging to see that our school breakfast programs are helping end hunger in the classroom, so students can concentrate on their classes."[12]

Unctuous rhetoric of this sort obscures a tectonic shift in personal responsibility. We can confidently stipulate that proper nutrition is a good thing and that we can agree on the desirability of feeding children wholesome meals. The real question is: Who is responsible for feeding them? Mothers and fathers? Or the taxpayers? Families, or Other People?

Increasingly, the answer is Other People.

This is not to suggest that there are not genuine problems among some dysfunctional families, but the problem is not widespread enough to justify the universalization of either free lunches or free breakfasts. Malnutrition is defined as "reduced health due to a chronic shortage of calories and nutriment." But there is very little evidence of poverty-induced malnutrition in the United States. Hunger is defined by the USDA as "the uneasy or painful sensation caused by lack of food," but it appears that nearly all "hunger" is "short-term and episodic rather than continuous." On a typical day, according to the government, fewer than half of one percent of Americans will experience hunger because of a lack of money.[13]*

In fact, multiple studies confirm that, on average, low-income children are quite well fed and there is little evidence of "under-nutrition."† Junk food is, of course, consumed at all income levels.

---

* Reports analyst Robert Rector: "Some 92 percent of those who experienced hunger in 2002 were adults, and only 8 percent were children. Overall, some 567,000 children, or 0.8 percent of all children, were hungry at some point in 2002. In a typical month, roughly one child in 400 skipped one or more meals because the family lacked funds to buy food. . . . Among poor children, 2.4 percent experienced hunger at some point in the year. Overall, most poor households were not hungry and did not experience food shortages during the year."

† Notes Rector, reliable data gathered by the government show that "the average nutriment consumption among the poor closely resembles that of the upper middle class. For example, children in families with incomes below the poverty level actually consume more meat than do children in families with incomes at 350 percent of the poverty level or higher (roughly $65,000 for a family of four in today's dollars). . . .

"It is widely believed that a lack of financial resources forces poor people to eat low quality diets that are deficient in nutriments and high in fat. However, survey data show that nutriment density (amount of vitamins, minerals, and protein per kilocalorie of food) does not vary by income class. Nor do the poor consume higher fat diets than do the middle class; the percentage of persons with high fat intake (as a share of total calories) is virtually the same for low-income and upper-middle-income persons. Overconsumption of calories in general, however, is a major problem among the poor, as it is within the general U.S. population."

But there is little evidence that poor children have been left out of benefiting from the nutritional advances of the last century. One measure: growth rates, height, and weight of children. Low-income 18- and 19-year-olds today are both taller and heavier than the average of the same age in the general American population in the late 1950s. Notes Rector, "Poor boys living today are one inch taller and some 10 pounds heavier than GIs of similar age during World War II, and nearly two inches taller and 20 pounds heavier than American doughboys back in World War I."[14]

Stigma? What Stigma?

School lunches are, however, only part of the shift toward free meals.

As the programs have grown, free or subsidized meals are no longer rationally related to feeding the hungry or those unable to provide for themselves; instead they are driven by an impulse to universalize the benefits, removing any lingering stigma, while spreading dependency as a virtue as widely as possible. In other words: Everybody should buy everybody's lunch! And breakfast too! (And did I mention dinner also would be nice?)

No program has grown more explosively than the program formerly known as food stamps.

In just two years, the number of people on food stamps rose by more than 10 million, while spending nearly doubled. On election day in 2008, 31 million people were on the rolls, at a cost to taxpayers of $39 billion in fiscal year 2008. Within two years, the number of recipients rose to 42.4 million and the federal 2011 budget projected spending of $75 billion.[15]

The 2009 stimulus bill helped open the floodgates by loosening restrictions on eligibility, even as its raised benefits increased spending. The legislation, for example, dropped requirements that able-bodied recipients without children had to work at least half-time to be eligible—a particular boon to failure-to-launch hipsters (about whom we'll talk more later). As significant as the cost and numbers are, the shift in public attitude has been equally dramatic, accompanied by media cheerleading for the loss of stigma once associated with food stamp usage. *The New York Times* chronicled the dawning age of dependency when it reported that food stamp dependence "has grown so rapidly in places so diverse that it is becoming nearly as ordinary as the groceries it buys."[16]

There were, of course, some minor, awkward glitches, including the story of a woman who "drove to the food stamp office in a Mercedes-Benz and word spread that she owned a $300,000 home loan-free. Since Ohio ignores the value of houses and cars, she qualified."

But, the *Times* reported, attitudes toward the program continued to improve as "across the small towns and rolling farmland outside Cincinnati, old disdain for the program has collided with new needs." Americans were learning to love the dole. Like other forms of dependency, food stamp usage is addictive. Despite claims that food stamps are a temporary, stopgap measure, according to the Heritage Foundation, "the majority of food stamp recipients at any given time are or will become long-term dependents. In fact, half of food stamp aid goes to individuals who have received aid for 8.5 years or more."[17]

Nevertheless, the program continues to expand under new management and with a new moniker, Food Share, that theoretically lessens the sting of the dole. The *Times* found that at least one quarter of the population in 239 counties across the country was dependent on the stamps. Among children, dependency was even more widespread. The story cited a recent study by Mark R. Rank, a professor at Washington University in St. Louis, who found that half of Americans—and a startling 90 percent of black children—received food stamps before they turned 20.[18]

Still it was not enough; the push to expand dependency continued apace.

"Although the program is growing at a record rate, the federal official who oversees it would like it to grow even faster," the *Times* reported, quoting Kevin Concannon, the undersecretary of Agriculture, who said, "I think the response to the program has been tremendous." (Of course this is "tremendous" only if you regard a massive increase in dependency as a cause for jubilation.)

But, he added, the federal government is "mindful that there are another 15, 16 million who could benefit." In other words, despite a nearly 33 percent increase in food stamp usage, he would not be satisfied unless it rose by yet another 39 percent—envisioning a country where as many as 57 million Americans rely on the taxpayers to buy their Doritos for them.

At least some institutions of higher learning have taken up the cause of spreading food stamp dependency. An investigation by the Web site the Daily Caller found that colleges around the country were actively steering students—many of them middle class—toward food stamps as a form of financial aid. Both Portland State and Pacific University in Oregon encouraged students to sign up for the stamps. Explained Portland State's Web site: "Being a college student is hard work! Not just academically, but financially too."[19] The school made the case for students jumping on the food stamp bandwagon: "As tuition increases, many students struggle to make ends meet. Sometimes grants and loans don't stretch far enough and students are forced to work low-paying jobs. For some, this still is not enough to get by. Having to choose between buying groceries or a $125 textbook is a tough decision that many students have been forced to make at some point in their college careers. As if taking a full class load wasn't stressful enough!"

The push on campuses appears to be paying off as food stamp use is rising among college students. Cato Institute budget analyst Tad DeHaven told the Daily Caller that he expects the food stamp program to continue to grow dramatically. "[It's] the mentality that, 'well, so and so is getting their share, so I should get my share as well,'" DeHaven said. "It's a quintessential example of people endeavoring to live at the expense of other people."

Hungry Hipsters

The success in breaking down old stigmas associated with mooching off the taxpayers was documented by the online magazine *Salon.com*. Salon created a minisensation when it published a story titled "Hipsters on Food Stamps," which reported on the ease with which middle- and upper-middle-class creative types shrugged off "old taboos" about combining freeloading with living large.[20]

Reported Salon: "Think of it as the effect of a grinding recession crossed with the epicurean tastes of young people as obsessed with food as previous generations were with music and sex. Faced with lingering unemployment, 20- and 30-somethings with college degrees and foodie standards are shaking off old taboos about who should get government assistance and discovering that government benefits can indeed be used for just about anything edible, including wild-caught fish, organic asparagus and triple-crème cheese."

By eliminating work requirements for able-bodied no-kids singles, the massive 2009 stimulus bill opened the door for yuppies to indulge their culinary passions courtesy of the taxpayer. The free federal cash, reported Salon, had instant appeal for "20- and 30-something creatives and young professionals" and, as a result, "the kinds of food markets that specialize in delectables like artisanal bread, heirloom tomatoes and grass-fed beef have seen significant upticks in food stamp payments among their typical shoppers."

This included a 30-year-old art grad student named Sarah

Magida and her partner Gerry Mak, a graduate of the University of Chicago, who said that about half of her friends are now on food stamps and told Salon of her delight when she discovered that "you can get anything" on the government stamps. Magida used food stamps to purchase "fresh produce, raw honey and fresh-squeezed juices from markets near her house in the neighborhood of Hampden, and soy meat alternatives and gourmet ice cream from a Whole Foods a few miles away."

"I'm eating better than I ever have before," she told Salon. "Even with food stamps, it's not like I'm living large, but it helps."

Magida then provided what could be the moocher mantra: "At first, I thought, 'Why should I be on food stamps?' Here I am, this educated person who went to art school, and there are a lot of people who need them more. But then I realized, I need them, too."

Part Three

AT THE TROUGH

I, Piggy Bank

✳   ✳   ✳

My 401(k) is down 30 percent, my employer just cut the match, and it looks like I may have to work until I'm seventy years old. I also pay for pensions to public employees who retired in their fifties.

I don't have enough money to go on vacation this year, but I paid my share of the federal government's $2.6 million grant to teach Chinese prostitutes to drink responsibly. I pay for bridges to nowhere.

I drive a 1997 Honda Accord, but I had to pay for my neighbor's $41,000 electric car. I also bailed out the United Auto Workers.

I contribute to my children's 529 college savings plan, but since I don't qualify for financial aid, I pay for other people's kids to go to school as well. I also pay for the sociology classes where I am sneered at for my lack of social conscience and denounced as the very essence of greed, racism, and environmental insensitivity.

I exercise regularly, watch my cholesterol, and pay for my own health insurance as well as copays and deductibles. I also pay for Other People's tonsillectomies, appendectomies, and occasional rhinoplasties. I pay taxes for Medicare, Medicaid, and various medical programs for poor children, and now I will get to subsidize the health care of several million more nonelderly, nonimpoverished Americans.

My small business just lost its line of credit, but I paid to bail out Citigroup, AIG, and Goldman Sachs, whose executives get bonuses bigger than my entire net worth.

I pay my mortgage, but I also pay to bail out banks that made risky loans and yuppies who have trouble paying $700,000 mortgages on their McMansions they bought with no down payments and adjustable-rate deals.

I pay for groceries for my family, but I also pay millionaire farmers not to grow stuff like rice. I buy dinner for more than 42 million food stamp recipients (although they now call it Food Shares). I also pay for school lunches. And breakfasts, since other parents apparently can't be expected to feed their kids. I get red meat once a week, but I pay for urban hipsters to buy organic salmon at Whole Foods.

I pay my electricity and gas bills, but I also pay for other people's air conditioning, cell phones, digital televisions, new windows, subsidized rent, and remodeling.

I pay for my daughter's ballet lessons, but I also pay for universities to develop computerized choreography programs that will help create "interactive dance performances with real-time audience interactions." I probably won't be able to make the show, since I'll be working.

I'm trying to save enough money in case I lose my job, but I pay for more than seventy different means-tested poverty programs.

Because I work hard and am successful, I am in the 10 percent of Americans who now pay more than 71 percent of the total federal income tax burden. The top 50 percent of earners pay 97.11 percent. In other words, the bottom half of American earners—theoretically 50 percent of the electorate—pay less than 3 percent of federal income taxes. I pay for them.

I pay property taxes, sales taxes, excise taxes, taxes on my phone, my cable, my water, state income taxes, Social Security, and Medicare taxes. I also help pay the bills for the nearly half of households who no longer pay any federal income tax. I also pay the bills for the 60 to 70 percent of households who receive more from the government than they pay in.

I expect no gratitude for any of this; it has been years since the term "provider" was a matter of societal respect and personal pride. I understand that the transfer of wealth from makers to takers is seen as morally purer than the efforts of those who created wealth in the first place.

I know my role.

I am the piggy bank.

Chapter 7

HARVESTING OPM

If transfer payments and subsidies were limited to low-income individuals, this would be a book merely about the welfare state. But the reliance on OPM extends far beyond the poor into corporate America, upper-income owners of beach homes, affluent farmers, public employees, and entitled yuppies who have developed the habit and expectation of mooching off others.

Even Hollywood has gotten in on the cash grab, convincing states to give moviemakers special tax breaks that are generally not extended to more mundane businesses whose employees do not have personal cosmetologists on speed dial.

The Glitziest Mooch

In Massachusetts, for example, taxpayers provide moviemakers millions of dollars in tax credits every year. Supporters justify the handouts by claiming that the productions create local jobs. The state, however, estimates that only 222 jobs were created by the program in 2009, at a cost to taxpayers of $325,000 apiece.[1]

But the tax credits ultimately weren't about the lighting technicians, security guards, and makeup artists who got temporary jobs catering to the celebrity elite. According to an analysis by the Associated Press, a quarter of the tax breaks handed over to the filmmakers in 2009 went to "cover the paychecks of millionaire Hollywood stars."[2] Under the Hollywood subsidy, producers are eligible for a Massachusetts tax credit equal to 25 percent of the production's costs. As it turned out, fully $82 million of the spending eligible for the film credits was used to pay out-of-state actors pulling down more than $1 million.*

Massachusetts is one of forty-three states offering inducements to movie and television production companies to shoot within their borders, part of the scramble to compete for a brief cameo by Johnny Depp or Angelina Jolie. A relatively recent phenomenon, the subsidies had risen to $1.5 billion by 2010, money that the Center on Budget and Policy Priorities states "otherwise could have been spent on public services like education, health care, public safety, and infrastructure. In 2009, that money would have paid for the salaries of 23,500 middle school teachers, 26,600 firefighters, and

---

* Reported the Associated Press: "Big money movies shot in Massachusetts in 2009 included 'The Fighter,' chronicling the career of Lowell boxer Micky Ward and starring Boston native Mark Wahlberg; 'The Social Network,' depicting the origin of Facebook, co-founded by Mark Zuckerberg in his Harvard dorm room in 2004; and the Ben Affleck movie 'The Town,' focusing on a Boston bank heist crew."

22,800 police patrol officers." In California alone, the subsidies cost the state $100 million a year.[3]

The median tax credit is worth about 25 cents for every dollar a Hollywood producer spends; but some states are far more generous: Alaska and Michigan offer 44 cents and 42 cents in credits respectively. This very sweet deal actually gets even sweeter, because film companies are often allowed to claim the credits even if they lose money. Better yet, some states make the credits "refundable."

The Center on Budget and Policy Priorities explains that it works this way: "If a producer lacks sufficient tax liability to use all of a *refundable* film tax credit, the state pays the producer the whole credit anyway, in effect giving the producer an outright cash grant. For example, suppose that a producer is awarded a film tax credit of $100,000 but has a pre-credit tax liability of only $50,000. A nonrefundable credit would reduce the producer's tax liability to $0 but leave it with $50,000 in unusable credits. If the tax credit is refundable, the state pays the producer $100,000, including the $50,000 in credits it otherwise could not use."*

In other words, the state transfers money from waitresses and truck drivers in Lowell to celebrity moviemakers in Beverly Hills.

Even among the makers of successful and profitable films, there is an entrenched sense of entitlement about this Glitterati Welfare. "If you take that away, I think production will leave the U.S.," producer Brian Oliver told *The New York Times*. Even though his production company can boast such hits as *Black Swan,* he complained that it "could not function without public money."[4]

---

* Another sweet deal: "Transferable" tax credits enable producers to sell their credits to a third party. The Center on Budget and Policy Priorities explains: "Often, those purchasers are financial services firms. Insurance companies find purchases of film tax credits especially profitable, since they can use them to reduce taxes on premiums. Through the end of fiscal year 2009, insurance companies had purchased about half of all transferred Massachusetts film tax credits, for example, and other financial institutions had purchased about a quarter of them."

But the Center on Budget and Policy Priorities concludes that the Hollywood subsidies are "wasteful, ineffective, and unfair."[5] Like many of the special-interest giveaways, the center concluded that the "benefits to the few are highly visible; the costs to the majority are hidden because they are spread so widely and detached from the subsidies."

Here we need to return to the larger question: How did we get to the point where taxpayers are required to subsidize Hollywood millionaires? By what standard of equity do we take money from schoolteachers and firefighters and transfer it (however indirectly) to Lindsay Lohan or Ben Affleck? And how does the Hollywood elite justify sticking those taxpayers with a tab? Could it be because so many others are doing the same thing?

If the Hollywood handouts illustrate the breadth of our moocher culture, modern American agriculture has come to symbolize the depth of its addictive power.

Harvesting OPM

As John Stossel surveyed the landscape of rip-offs, trough feeders, and scam jobs, he noticed one of the paradoxes at the heart of Moocher Nation: Today's biggest welfare queens, wrote Stossel, were probably farmers. "This is odd," noted the Fox News correspondent, "because farmers were once the most self-sufficient of Americans."[6] It is, indeed, remarkable what several generations of dependency can do.

No discussion of corporate welfare or of mooching in general would be complete without the fiasco of agricultural subsidies, the bureaucratic blizzard of overlapping programs that include direct payments, marketing loans, so-called counter-cyclical payments, conservation subsidies, insurance, disaster aid, export subsidies, and agricultural research. Together, they have become one of the largest middle- and upper-class welfare programs in the country. Between 1995 and 2009, federal taxpayers paid out a quarter of a trillion dollars in agricultural subsidies.[7]

While aid to farmers is romanticized as necessary to save family farms run by rugged individualists at the mercy of the next plague of locusts, the reality is far different. From 1995 to 2009, 73 percent of the total aid went to just 10 percent of the recipients, generally some of the country's largest and richest farms.[8] Most of the subsidies, in fact, go to farms with net worths of $2 million or more and average incomes of $200,000 a year.* While the average total payment to big farms was $445,127 over that period, the bottom 80 percent of farmers received just $8,682.

Stories of the rich and well heeled feeding at the farm welfare trough have become deservedly legend. ABC's Sam Donaldson famously pocketed thousands of federal dollars in "wool and mohair" subsidies because he raised sheep and goats on his ranch. Like so many of the other recipients of the federal aid, Donaldson had the grace to admit that the payments were a "horrible mess," but he rationalized his acceptance of them by comparing the payments to the home mortgage deduction, telling Stossel: "As long as the law is on the books, it's appropriate to take advantage of it."[9]

He was hardly alone in that respect. Stossel noted that some other affluent moochers included basketball star Scott Pippen

---

* Reports the Environmental Working Group: "Despite claims of reform . . . six of the top 10 recipients of commodity payments in 2009 were in the top 20 in both 2007 and 2008. Of the top 20, 8 were in the list all three years, and three more were there in 2009 and one other year. In contrast to the public fury over billion-dollar bailouts of Wall Street banks, all 20 top subsidy recipients in 2009 received more than $1 million each, several with multimillion-dollar hauls. And this is only one year's worth of corporate handouts that have gone on for decades. Three of these repeat offenders did quite well in 2009. California's SJR Farms took in $2,069,453, Louisiana's Balmoral Farming Partnership received $1,910,834 and Arizona's Gila River Farms collected $1,711,444."

($131,575), TV mogul Ted Turner ($176,077), and David Rocke-feller ($352,187).

The byzantine network of payments, subsidies, and transfers have many of the worst elements of both bailouts and welfare, but as the Environmental Working Group points out, comparisons with the agricultural subsidies are unfair to both bailouts and welfare. "After all, with bailouts taxpayers usually get their money back (often with interest)," notes the group's president Ken Cook, "while welfare recipients are subjected to harsh means-testing, time-limited benefits and a work requirement. . . . None of those characteristics apply to America's farm subsidy system, a *sui generis* contraption that might have sprung from the fevered anti-government fantasies of tea party cynics if Congress hadn't thought it up first."[10]

An investigative series in *The Washington Post* in 2006 concluded that the subsidy programs have "little basis in fairness or efficiency." Beginning as a "safety net" program during the Great Depression, the farm programs have morphed into an intricate network of payments, subsidies, and transfer payments that by 2005 were nearly 50 percent more than the federal government's payments to welfare families—at a time when farm profits were at near-record levels.[11]

Embarrassed

Perhaps most striking about the billions of dollars in farm payments, besides the extraordinary cost and economic inefficiency, are the number of recipients who frankly admit they are embarrassed they are taking the cash (but take it anyway). Several farmers told *The Washington Post* they were chagrined at taking offers of unearned and unmerited federal money for disasters they didn't suffer or for crops they never grew but, in the end, the stigma was too light and the draw was simply too strong.

When *The Washington Post,* for example, profiled a 67-year-old contractor named Donald R. Matthews who owned an eighteen-acre property in the "heart of rice country," the paper noted that even though Matthews was not a farmer and didn't intend to be one, he was pocketing $1,300 a year in "direct payments" because "years ago the land used to grow rice."

"I don't agree with the government's policy," Matthews told the *Post.* "They give all of this money to landowners who don't even farm, while real farmers can't afford to get started. It's wrong." But when Matthews tried to give the money back he was told that it would just go to other nonfarming landowners who had never planted a seed—landowners like the 87-year-old woman who had pocketed $191,000 over the previous decade, or the Houston surgeon who had gotten nearly $490,709. "I thought, heck, why should I do that? I wasn't going to give it to somebody else to put in their pocket." He uses the money to fund scholarships. But he still doesn't feel right about it.

"Still, I get money I don't think I'm entitled to," he told the newspaper.

Between 2000 and 2006, reported the *Post,* taxpayers paid out at least $1.3 billion in subsidies, like the ones to Matthews for rice and other crops "to individuals who do no farming at all."* In other words they paid them for precisely . . . nothing.[12]

As the *Post* documented, billions of dollars are paid with little logic or justification, and no legitimate standard of need. One Illinois

---

* Reported the *Post:* "The program that pays Matthews was the central feature of a landmark 1996 farm law that was meant to be a break with the farm handouts of the past. . . . Instead of cutting, Congress ended up expanding the program, now known as direct and countercyclical payments. A program intended to cost $36 billion over seven years instead topped $54 billion. . . . In fact, so many landowners and farmers are collecting money on their former ricelands—$37 million last year alone—that the acres no longer used for rice outnumber the planted ones."

farmer profiled in the series who grossed nearly $500,000 a year was still eligible for payments of $120,000. "It's embarrassing," one prosperous farmer told the paper. "My government is basically saying I am incompetent and need help." Over the previous five years, the family had pocketed $357,000 in government money.[13]

Then there are beneficiaries of "disaster" aid.

Money for Nothing . . .

Dutch immigrant Nico de Boer was neither needy nor disadvantaged by any conceivable definitions of those terms. He owned a thousand acres of land in Texas, 650 cows that produced 3 million gallons of milk a month, and all the trappings of success and affluence: "a BMW in the driveway, a swimming pool, and two more farms in neighboring counties."[14]

In February 2003, the Space Shuttle *Challenger* exploded in the skies near De Boer's ranch. He suffered no damage and never saw any debris—but he was still entitled to $40,000 in "disaster compensation" even though the nearest debris was probably at least ten miles from any of his cows. Reported the *Post*: "The money came from the U.S. Department of Agriculture as part of the Livestock Compensation Program, originally intended as a limited helping hand for dairy farmers and ranchers hurt by drought." Instead, livestock owners in Henderson County, Texas, collected $751,083 "despite no shuttle damage."

"The livestock program was a joke. We had no losses," De Boer told the *Post*. "I don't know what Congress is thinking sometimes." But despite his reluctance, De Boer, like the other ranchers, cashed the checks: "If there is money available, you might as well take it. You would be a fool not to."

Mrs. Davey (the British moocher mom) could hardly have said it better.

My Favorite Crop

The point to be emphasized once again is that this large-scale mooching has little or nothing to do with genuine need. Of the $1.2 billion paid out in the first two years of the Livestock Compensation Program, for instance, the *Post* reported that "$635 million went to ranchers and dairy farmers in areas where there was moderate drought or none at all." There was barely a pretense that the cash was related to genuine misfortune. "None of the ranchers were required to prove they suffered an actual loss. The government simply sent each of them a check based on the number of cattle they owned."[15]

Reported the *Post*: "In one county in northern Texas, ranchers collected nearly $1 million for an ice storm that took place a year and a half before the livestock program was even created. In Washington State, ranchers in one county received $1.6 million for an earthquake that caused them no damage. In Wisconsin, a winter snowstorm triggered millions of dollars more. For hundreds of ranchers from East Texas to the Louisiana border, the shuttle explosion opened the door to about $5 million, records show."[16]

The system has also become a classic case of government favoritism. A handful of crops from certain states reap the bounty of federal generosity: More than 70 percent of farm subsidies went to support just five crops: corn, wheat, cotton, rice, and soybeans. In 2009, the Environmental Working Group (EWG) noted, "a full 60 percent of farm subsidies flowed to states represented by senators serving on the Senate Committee on Agriculture, Nutrition and Forestry."[17] Hardly a coincidence.

Much of the income transfer is masked by opaque bureaucratese—Orwellian jargon that seems designed specifically to confuse outsiders. A case in point is the so-called loan deficiency program. "Despite its name," noted *The Washington Post*, "it is neither a loan nor, in many cases, payment for a deficiency. It is just cash paid to farmers when market prices dip below the government-set minimum, or floor, if only for a single day." The cost to taxpayers in 2006: $4.8 billion.[18]

Then there is insurance. Even after the passage of Obamacare in 2010, the EWG said, "most crops could fairly be said to have better coverage than many people in this country—and it's single-payer coverage. . . . Taxpayer subsidized crop insurance is available to farmers if their crop is eligible for coverage in their area, and it provides, at no cost, 50 percent catastrophic coverage to farmers. . . . Small wonder that since 1995, America's public option-only crop insurance program has cost taxpayers $35 billion."[19]

Despite all of this cash, the programs do not appear to achieve many of the goals claimed for the programs. Some of the subsidies are designed to raise farmer income by propping up the prices of their crops; in reality, they often depress those prices by encouraging overproduction.[20] They also have the unintended consequence of driving legitimate farmers off the land, after landowners discover they can make more by doing nothing than by growing things.

The *Post* reported that landlords "have evicted the tenants from land they had farmed for years. Then the landowners can collect the checks themselves, even if they do not farm."

"As soon as they figured they could take the payments, they said, 'I don't need you anymore,'" one farmer told the *Post*. "They were renting me land for $40 an acre, but they could get $125 an acre from the government."[21]

Perhaps not surprisingly, the billions of dollars in corporate welfare have failed to slow the exodus of Americans from farms.

Indeed, the counties most dependent on the subsidies had the weakest job growth and worst population losses. A study by the Federal Reserve Bank of Kansas City concluded, "Farm payments appear to create dependency on even more payments, not new engines of economic growth."

The EWG notes this one signal of success: "One thing government subsidies reliably produce, other than ingratitude and a sense of entitlement among their recipients, is a demand for more subsidies."

> Sure enough, the resulting 2007 energy bill mandated American drivers to put 15 billion gallons of corn ethanol in their tanks every year by 2015, with accompanying tax breaks to gasoline blenders that already approach the $5 billion spent each year on automatic direct payments. Since not even those government props have been sufficient to maintain profitability, the corn ethanol industry has been laying siege to Capitol Hill and the White House to increase the mix of ethanol in gasoline by 50 percent. Next will come a demand to expand the 15 billion gallon annual mandate to 20 billion gallons or more of corn ethanol.[22]

Because, of course, whatever the government does for you—it is never enough.

Flood of Money

Middle- and upper-class welfare is not limited to farm subsidies. Perhaps the most dramatic transfer payments go to the owners of pricey beachfront properties. If the definition of *insanity* is doing the same thing over and over again and expecting a different outcome, the National Flood Insurance Program would be Exhibit A.*

Consider Alabama's Dauphin Island: From 1979 through 2005, the island was hammered six times by hurricanes, which destroyed about five hundred pricey vacation home and rental properties. Yet, as *The Washington Post* noted, "owners keep building back. . . . And the island has received more than $21 million in federal flood payments to help spur development."[23]

Not surprisingly, the federal program is broke, looking for a $19 billion federal bailout. One could easily argue that the flood program is designed to fail: it pays virtually every claim, doesn't raise premiums after multiple claims, and promises to keep covering homes that have been destroyed over and over again. It can also be argued that the program is designed precisely to reward irresponsible behavior, like providing a subsidy for pyromaniacs to buy matches.

When *USA Today* examined the program, it found that more than 19,600 owners of houses and commercial property had actually pocketed more in federal insurance payments than the total actual value of their properties. For example, the program paid one Alabama homeowner $2.3 million in claims, even though the house was worth only $153,000; a Houston home worth just $116,000 generated $1.6 million in claims. Meanwhile, homeowners continue to rebuild over and over again, benefiting from big discounts in insurance rates—insurance that would either never be written by a private company or would cost dramatically more to reflect the actual risk and claims history. The cost of the discounts: at least $1 billion a year—the taxpayer's gift to improvident beach dwellers.[24]

In all, 5.5 million properties are covered by the program, which

---

* The analogy has been frequently made. In a story on the program, *USA Today* quoted environmentalist David Conrad of the National Wildlife Federation as saying: "It does seem to fit Albert Einstein's definition of insanity—to somehow expect something different when you do the same thing over and over again." (Thomas Frank, "Insurance Underwater," *USA Today*, August 26, 2010.)

provides flood protection up to $350,000 for single-family homes and $1 million for commercial properties. The Institute for Policy Integrity, affiliated with New York University's law school, notes that the "insurance subsidies are a direct transfer, through the program, from taxpayers to the holders of these policies."[25]

The beneficiaries of all this largesse? Rich areas, like Longboat Keys, Florida, and Hilton Head Island, South Carolina, which *USA Today* found had "some of the largest numbers of second homes and rentals getting the discounts."[26] In other words, it is taxpayer-subsidized insurance for the beautiful people . . . or at least the fortunate few who have managed to get other people to bankroll their affluent lifestyles.

The Institute for Policy Integrity notes that there are occasional claims that the program primarily benefits poor regions of the country. But the institute reports that more careful analysis calls those claims into question. Hurricanes Rita and Katrina in 2005 skew the historic numbers dramatically. The institute's researchers found that if 2005 is excluded from the decade 1998–2008, "the wealthiest counties in the country filed 3.5 times more claims and received over a billion dollars more in claim payments than the poorest counties." Their conclusion: "Taxpayer-subsidized [flood] claims thus represent a significant wealth transfer from middle-income counties to relatively wealthy and poor counties."[27] Nationwide, the median value of a single-family home is roughly $160,000. But the Congressional Budget Office (CBO) says that more than 40 percent of the coastal properties benefiting from subsidies of their insurance rates because they were grandfathered into the federal insurance program are worth more than a half million dollars; 12 percent are worth more than a million dollars. Nearly a quarter of the homes in the CBO analysis were vacation homes. "While the CBO analysis is not exhaustive," the institute notes, "it strongly suggests that the benefits of subsidized flood insurance provided by the NFIP accrue primarily to wealthy households."[28]

This, of course, makes perfect sense. Who, after all, is most likely able to afford oceanfront properties? As the institute points out, "The most expensive homes are those directly on the beach, followed by homes with a view of the ocean, then those within walking distance of the ocean, and finally those homes without easy access to the water." The only thing that ruins the view from the deck is the prospect of being flooded out, the financial cost of which ocean-viewing property owners, mai tai in hand, do not have to worry about, thanks to taxpayers who likely have to make do with more prosaic views.

Many of the subsidized rich could, of course, afford this lifestyle themselves. Others might think twice about building in floodplains or in coastal areas where their investments would be swept away if they had to do it on their own dime. If they were forced to pay full price for their insurance or bear the financial risk of their decisions, presumably, many of the subsidized ocean dwellers would choose different, more prudent venues. But as long as the federal government offers the cut-rate policies, why not take them? The lure of government cash is as powerful for a celebrity building a dream home on the Florida coast as it is for the farmer pocketing disaster aid for losses he didn't suffer, or Aunt Zeituni taking advantage of government handouts. *If they are giving away money, who am I to say no?*

In the case of flood insurance, there is an additional wrinkle: Like farmers and other corporate moochers, the owners of beach homes tend to have the sort of political juice needed to keep a boondoggle of this size and scope afloat. Thus, despite the ongoing transfer of wealth from middle-income taxpayers to wealthy beach communities, recipients can still count on defenders to justify the payments on "compassionate" grounds.

But does "compassion" really describe why a Mississippi home worth just $69,900 could be flooded thirty-four times and generate $663,000 in insurance payments?[29] Wouldn't "delusional" be more appropriate? Federal taxpayers are subsidizing both the homeowner's lifestyle and his refusal to acknowledge the realities. But the subsidies keep on rolling in with the tide.

For the beneficiaries of the cut-rate insurance—who can afford to have repairmen on speed dial after every flooding—this is a sweet deal. But it spells financial disaster for the taxpayers. "The program, as currently structured," says the Institute for Policy Integrity, "will never repay its debt."[30]

Translation: The taxpayers will get to bail them out as well.

Moocher's Dilemma II

✣ ✣ ✣

Some thought experiments:

☐ If you steal $8,000 in cash from your neighbor, it is theft. The act is universally condemned as an instance of dishonesty as well as breaking the law, and if caught you are likely to be jailed.

☐ If you compel your neighbor to pay $8,000 so you can buy a house (via the transfer of wealth through tax credits), it is perfectly legal. The transfer is celebrated as both socially beneficial and necessary for the recovery of the housing market.

☐ If you steal a car, it is a crime. The theft is not only constrained by the power of law, it is also clearly immoral and, thus, condemned by social norms.

☐ If you force your neighbor to buy you a car (via Cash for Clunkers or tax subsidies for hybrids and electric vehicles), it is perfectly legal and applauded by the political class as stimulative.

Explain the differences: Why is the appropriation of another's property condemned in the first and third instances, but embraced as a matter of public policy and social good in the other two? Is this a distinction without a difference? Or does plunder under the color of law make it no longer plunder?

Bonus:

☐ You arrive at a potluck dinner empty-handed, but you proceed to feed deep at all the tables, groaning under homemade quiches, pot pies, casseroles, and desserts. You are considered a freeloader.

☐ You pay no money in federal income tax, but you benefit from hundreds of federal programs, including national defense and dozens of antipoverty programs that pay for your housing, transportation, heating, and food, and provide you with cash. What should you be considered?

Chapter 8

CRONY CAPITALISM (BIG BUSINESS AT THE TROUGH)

In the HBO series *The Wire*, the ability to influence power is referred to colloquially as "suckage." Those who have it stand to gain favors, indulgences, and protection from the political class; those who lack sufficient "suckage" are left out in the cold. The concept may go by different names but the principle dominates the nation's capital, giving rise to a new aristocracy of clout.

Consider the new Lobbying Class: They neither sow nor build; they manipulate; they curry favor with legislators; they cajole regulators; they appease administrations; and they multiply as government expands. Even as the rest of the economy stagnated, the new class has flourished. A machinist might find his job outsourced to India or China, but for the seeker of political clout all roads lead to Washington, D.C.

"Lay out a picnic, you get ants," explains the Cato Institute's David Boaz, "hand out more wealth through government, you get lobbyists."[1] As *The Washington Post* noted in 2008, the explosion in the lobbying industry was "an extension of the growth and reach of government," which increasingly "has its tentacles in every aspect of American life and commerce." As a result, "No serious industry or interest can function without monitoring, and at least trying to manipulate, Washington's decision makers."[2]

Although the Great Bailout of 2008–09 defined a new high-water mark, corporate cronyism is responsible for the transfer of tens of billions of dollars of OPM every year. The influence lobby employs hundreds of thousands and pays out billions of dollars in salaries and fees. The list of corporate welfare queens reads like a *Who's Who of American Capitalism*: Pfizer, Boeing, General Electric, Archer Daniels Midland, Goldman Sachs, AT&T, AIG, and General Motors. They employ vast armies of favor seekers who lobby for bailouts, pork, tax credits, mandates, waivers, and even new regulations on their own industries.

One of the dirty little secrets in the culture of "suckage" is that many in business and the lobbying class, including those who espouse free market principles, actually like Big Government. In his letter to shareholders after the 2008 election, General Electric's CEO, Jeffrey Immelt, wrote that the Democratic victories that year meant the economy had been "reset."

"The interaction between government and business will change forever," he explained. "In a reset economy, the government will be a regulator; and also an industry policy champion, a financier, and a key partner."[3] He could have been writing a manifesto for the new corporatism in which business looked not only for subsidies, handouts, and cash to pad their bottom lines, but also for rules, regulations, and bureaucratic trip wires that benefit companies like GE.

Given the usual complaints about such regulations from business, this might seem counterintuitive, but many of the largest companies actually welcome the new regimes. More regulations make it harder for competitors to horn in on market share because the very complexity and opacity of the spiderwebs of rules give insiders special access to the keys to the kingdom. Since the 1970s, "public choice" theory economists have recognized that "regulation is acquired by the industry and is designed and operated primarily for its benefit."[4] This is known as "capture theory," which describes how business seizes and uses the regulatory regimes for its own bottom-line benefit and is far from hostile to government intervention. Capture theory explains how the push for ever-increasing regulation "is influenced by the incentives of legislators seeking campaign funding, bureaucrats seeking to expand their budgets and prestige, and business interests seeking advantages over their competitors."[5]

Only Little People (and Companies) Pay Taxes

General Electric's coziness with power and its ability to work the system has paid off handsomely for the company. Despite global profits topping $14 billion in 2010, the company managed to pay minimal federal corporate taxes.*

While other businesses and individuals struggle with paying income and corporate taxes, GE has managed to turn the tax code into a giant engine of corporate welfare, largely by pulling the levers of political power. "Over the last decade, G.E. has spent tens of

---

* *The New York Times* originally reported that the company had paid no federal tax at all and was actually able to tap the U.S. Treasury for a "tax benefit of $3.2 billion." But this was later called into question by analyses that suggested that GE paid a minimal amount of 2010 taxes. (Allan Sloan and Jeff Gerth, "The Truth about GE's Tax Bill," *Fortune*, April 4, 2011.)

millions of dollars to push for changes in tax law, from more generous depreciation schedules on jet engines to 'green energy' credits for its wind turbines," reported *The New York Times*. The corporation's success in winning special tax benefits has proven exceptionally valuable for both executives and shareholders.[6]

GE's executives understand where all this munificence comes from, spending millions on lobbying and besieging Washington at the first sign that the taxpayer largesse might be in jeopardy. In 2008, when the corporate giant was briefly threatened with a loss of some of the tax favors, for example, "the company came out in full force. G.E. officials worked with dozens of financial companies to send letters to Congress and hired a bevy of outside lobbyists."

The *Times* recounted this touching vignette:

> The head of its tax team, Mr. Samuels, met with Representative Charles B. Rangel, then chairman of the Ways and Means Committee, which would decide the fate of the tax break. As he sat with the committee's staff members outside Mr. Rangel's office, Mr. Samuels dropped to his knee and pretended to beg for the provision to be extended—a flourish made in jest, he said through a spokeswoman.

Whether in jest or not, Rangel reversed his position and decided to back the tax break sought by GE. The next month, reported the *Times*, "Mr. Rangel and Mr. Immelt stood together . . . as G.E. announced that its foundation had awarded $30 million to New York City schools, including $11 million to benefit various schools in Mr. Rangel's district."

Few companies have more lucrative "suckage."

Getting in Line

As government increasingly tries to pick winners and losers in the marketplace, the stakes continue to rise. Journalist Timothy Carney notes, "When government is discussing making some products (such as health insurance) mandatory, some (such as the incandescent light bulb) illegal, some (such as a trip to the tanning bed) more heavily taxed, some (such as wind-mills) more heavily subsidized, and granting others (such as biologic drugs) lengthy government-enforced monopolies, you can expect businesses to lobby up. . . . Even if Washington isn't threatening your industry, but is instead only handing out goodies, you still suffer by not investing in K Street, because your competitors will just get your share of the loot."[7]

Not only has the allure of billions of taxpayer dollars changed the rules and expectations of corporate America, but also the dollars have proven to be highly addictive. "Once executives get a taste of corporate welfare, they want more," notes Barry Ritholtz. "Do you have any idea *how hard it is* to earn $30 billion in a year? Flying commercial—or even driving—to Washington, DC, for an afternoon of hostile Q&A is a lot easier than having your company make $30 billion. The return on investment (ROI) on the day trip is *fantastic*."[8]

Even iconic and profitable companies like Disney have gotten in on the rush. In 2008, *The Washington Post* devoted a lengthy profile to the Mouse's campaign to tap in to hundreds of millions of dollars of corporate welfare. To access the stash, the *Post* detailed, the company planned to "remake its lobbying capabilities on a man-to-the-moon-like scale." The goal: $200 million in taxpayer money to promote tourism. "Getting taxpayers to underwrite overseas commercials had been the travel industry's Holy Grail for decades," reported the *Post*, and the industry was prepared to pay hand-somely for the subsidy.[9] In the 2006 campaign alone, the lodging, tourism, gambling, and recreation industries donated more than $20 million to federal candidates in the hope that, in return, grateful politicians would quadruple the amount of money the government spent to promote their businesses. With the strong support of Senate Majority Leader Harry Reid (D-Nev.), they succeeded. The Travel Promotion Act was signed into law in March 2010.[10]

Strictly speaking, none of this is new. The modern-day lobbying class has historical antecedents, most notably the class of courtiers who danced attendance on princes, seeking their favor and avoiding their frowns. But it is a type that flourishes only when power is concentrated and when kissing up pays more handsomely than doing or making. And kissing up to power pays richly indeed. A well-connected Washington lobbyist can expect to be paid twice, even three times, what he or she could make working for government and, as a result, reported *The Washington Post*, "government is now viewed by many on Capitol Hill as a steppingstone to a lucrative career in bending government to the whims of paying clients." Increasingly the industry of influence peddling has become a sort of shadow government, complete with "a bureaucracy, with its own language, its own peculiar ways of doing business and, most important, its own instinct to survive."[11]

Again, this is a familiar pattern. Economist Mancur Olson described the shift in the values of cultures that are destined for stagnation and decline: "Every society . . . gives greater rewards to the fittest—the fittest for *that* society. . . . If a society mainly rewards production of the capacity to satisfy those with whom one engages in free exchange, it stimulates the development of productive traits." On the other hand, if a society rewards clout and political juice, and politics replaces productivity as the source of prosperity, Olson noted drily, "this encourages the development of different attitudes and attributes."[12]

The result is not a kinder and gentler society. "Competition about the division of income is not any nicer than competition to produce or to please customers," wrote Olson. "The gang fight is fully as rough as the individual duel, and the struggle of special interest groups generates no magnanimity or altruism."

The Squeeze

In the fall of 2010, a lobbyist checked his voice mail and found a message from a then-powerful member of Congress.

> This is, uh, Eleanor Norton. Congresswoman Eleanor Holmes Norton. Uh, I noticed that you have given to, uh, other colleagues on the Transportation and Infrastructure Committee. I am a, um, senior member, a 20-year veteran and am chair of the subcommittee on Economic Development, Public Buildings and Emergency Management. I'm handling the largest economic development project in the United States now, the Homeland Security Compound of three buildings being built on the, uh, old St. Elizabeth's hospital site in the District of Columbia along with, uh, 15 other, uh, sites here for, that are part of the stimulus.
>
> I was, frankly, uh, uh, surprised to see that we don't have a record, so far as I can tell, of your having given to me despite my, uh, long and deep, uh, work. In fact, it's been my major work, uh, on the committee and subcommittee it's been essentially in your sector. I am, I'm simply candidly calling to ask for a contribution. As the senior member of the, um, committee and a subcommittee chair, we have [chuckles] obligations to raise, uh, funds . . . we particularly,

uh, need, uh, contributions, particularly those of us who have the seniority and chairmanships and are in a position to raise the funds.[13]

It was as close to a pure shakedown as you could come without actually breaking the law, but what was most striking about the call was how unshocking it really was. "If you've been paying attention," wrote longtime Washington insider Bill Kristol, "you know this is what politics in Washington, D.C., has come to. If you set up a casino of welfare statism, crony capitalism, and big government liberalism, this is what you're going to get."

Offense and Defense

In fairness, much of the lobbying explosion is defensive, part of the push-pull between currying favor and fending off damaging political interventions. In the halls of corporate America, the story of Microsoft is a cautionary tale. Perhaps assuming that its success would speak for itself without paying court to the powers in Washington, the software giant made no effort to mount a serious political presence. In 1999, the Clinton Justice Department smacked the firm with a massive antitrust suit that would eventually cost Microsoft billions of dollars and force it to change the way it did business. "Before then," noted *The Washington Post*, "it had mostly ignored the nation's capital."[14]

Few big firms make that mistake anymore, nor can they afford to. In recent years, Realtors ramped up their lobbying efforts, hoping both for bailouts and to fend off various antihousing measures (like the elimination of the home mortgage deduction). And as health care reform loomed, Big Pharma dramatically stepped up its own courtship of government.* As a result, notes Timothy Carney, "Every reform proposal with significant congressional backing represented corporate welfare for the drug makers. This is why the drug makers ran advertisements supporting 'reform.'"[15] This story could be told in industry after industry.

Out in the Cold

In Moocher America, success often turns on who you know. Chrysler bond holders discovered the downside of cronyism when they were forced to take a much bigger hit than the politically well-connected United Auto Workers when the government bailed out the company.[16] After the government takeover of General Motors, nonunion workers at supplier Delphi discovered the same thing.

In an extraordinary and unprecedented move, the federal government took over Delphi's pension plans at a cost of more than $6 billion, a move that potentially put taxpayers on the hook for the Pension Benefit Guaranty Corporation's growing deficit. The bailout marked a sharp reversal for the feds, who had insisted that Delphi and GM cover some of the costs and who had relied on GM's promise to cover the union plan if needed.[17] But, as *The New York Times* noted, the bailout had an additional "unusual twist."

"Normally, when a company pension fund is taken over by the government, workers may lose part of their benefits because pension insurance is limited. But it appears in Delphi's case that one group of workers and retirees will be spared cuts—the ones represented by the U.A.W."[18]

---

* According to the Center for Responsive Politics, the "Pharmaceutical/Health Products industry spent more on lobbying since 1998 than any other industry." (www.opensecrets.org)

Under pressure from the Obama administration, GM "topped up" the pension benefits for union members who might otherwise have seen their payouts shrink. The government-owned car company agreed to make up the estimated $4.3 billion pension shortfall for union workers who had been with Delphi as of 1999, but pointedly declined to do the same for the $2.5 billion pension deficit for Delphi's nonunion retirees.

Nonunion Delphi retirees were also out of luck when it came to health and life insurance. "Thus," wrote Carl Horowitz of the National Legal and Policy Center, "some 15,000 former administrators, purchasing managers, engineers, bookkeepers and other white-collar employees, many with the company for decades, are being hung out to dry."[19]

"The U.S. government is taking care of a select group of people and tossing the rest of us under the bus," Peter Beiter, a retired financial manager, told the *Times*.[20]

"These people are getting a first-hand lesson in the drawbacks of not being politically connected," noted Horowitz.[21] Columnist Nolan Finley of *The Detroit News* took the lesson to heart. In the new economic order, workers fell into two categories, "those who are worthy of the president's energies, and those who aren't."[22]

The division between those favored by the government and those who find themselves out in the cold, wrote Finley, was not determined by "what they do or whether they slip their feet into wingtips or steel-toed boots in the morning. His sole interest is in whether they have a union card in their wallet."

He could just as easily have said that the government's favor was determined by those who had "suckage," and those who lacked it.

Green Mooching

So-called green energy has proven a fertile field for the next generation of corporate welfare as the federal government steps up its efforts to single out favored companies for tax benefits and political blessing.

In August 2010, for example, President Obama visited a "clean energy" company, which he praised for "pointing the country toward a brighter economic future." He backed up the kind words with federal dollars. In January 2010, his administration had announced that ZBB Energy Corporation was one of 183 recipients of "clean energy tax credits" worth $14 million.

"As it happens," *The Wall Street Journal* noted the next day, "Mr. Obama couldn't have chosen a better company to demonstrate the risks that taxpayers are taking with their billions in green stimulus investment. . . . Since going public in June of 2007, ZBB has been hemorrhaging money. It explained it had a 'cumulative deficit' of $44.1 million and informed shareholders that it 'anticipates incurring continuing losses.'"[23]

Less than a month later, the company announced that its losses had widened and that they "reported no sales in the quarter just ended."[24]

Other grants of taxpayer largesse appear to be somewhat more incestuous. On the list of tax credits for green companies, for instance, the administration included only one window company: Serious Materials, an especially well-connected corporation. Serious won plaudits from Vice President Joe Biden, who credited the company with "inspiring a better tomorrow," and from the president himself, who praised the company for "producing some of the most energy-efficient windows in the world."

"This," noted John Stossel, "must be one very special company." Indeed.

As Stossel later reported, Cathy Zoi, the federal official who was appointed in April 2009 to oversee "$16.8 billion in stimulus funds, much of it for weatherization programs that benefit Serious," was married to Robin Roy, "who happens to be vice president of 'policy' at Serious Windows."[25*]

The federal government's inability to pick winners or substitute its judgment for that of the marketplace was illustrated by its Cash for Clunkers program, which was partly intended to help bail out the automakers and partly to meet green energy goals. On both counts it failed, while transferring $3 billion from the taxpayers to buyers of new cars. Under the program, car buyers could receive a direct subsidy of up to $4,500 for trading in an old car and buying a more fuel-efficient new car. In an orgy of green piety, the older—often perfectly usable—used car was then crushed.

The program, wrote journalist Carney, "captured every aspect of Obamanomics: big government, high spending, running up debt, rewarding special interests, claiming environmental benefit, claiming economic stimulus and displaying ignorance of basic economics."[26]

On a superficial level, Clunkers was a success, taking credit for the sale of about 360,000 cars in July and August of 2009. But in a working paper for the National Bureau of Economic Research, Atif Mian and Amir Sufi concluded that almost all of the sales were "pulled forward from the very near future; the effect of the program on auto purchases is almost completely reversed by as early as

---

* A spokesman for Serious insisted the company had nothing to hide: "Robin Roy had worked for us long before Cathy [Zoi] was offered that job." Quipped Stossel: "Of all the window companies in America, maybe it's a coincidence that the one which gets presidential and vice presidential attention and a special tax credit is one whose company executives give thousands of dollars to the Obama campaign and where the policy officer spends nights at home with the Energy Department's weatherization boss."

March 2010—only seven months after the program ended." Not only was the program's effect extraordinarily short-lived, they concluded, but they could "find no evidence of an effect on employment, house prices, or household default rates in cities with higher exposure to the program."[27]

Concluded columnist Jeff Jacoby: "When all is said and done, Cash for Clunkers was a deplorable exercise in budgetary wastefulness, asset destruction, environmental irrelevance, and economic idiocy. Other than that, it was a screaming success."[28]

The Biggest Piggy

No story of crony capitalism would be complete without a mention of Archer Daniels Midland (ADM), a company whose pursuit of clout and special favor made it almost a cliché of corporate mooching. What makes ADM so extraordinary has been its success in padding its bottom line in good times and in bad, through Democratic and Republican administrations alike. ADM greased the wheels of political influence with such abandon that John Stossel named them the Biggest Piggy, despite the fierce competition from other corporate welfare queens.[29]

ADM's relentless advocacy of government support for ethanol has been described as "a sad torrid affair of crony capitalism and green fantasies."[30] As such, it is something of a template for much of the crony capitalism that followed. Dwayne Andreas, ADM's longtime CEO, orchestrated decades worth of government favoritism that benefited his company, beginning with Jimmy Carter and extending through the Bush years. He lavished campaign contributions on politicians of both parties, seamlessly moving from supporting Hubert Humphrey to Richard Nixon to George H. W. Bush to Bill Clinton.

Carter had exempted gasohol from taxation; the first Bush exempted ethanol from the Clean Air Act; Clinton repealed Bush's exemption, but rewarded Andreas for his support by imposing the country's first ethanol mandate.[31]

ADM also benefits richly from federally mandated minimum prices for sugar because the policy encourages huge companies like Coca-Cola to buy corn sweetener (sold by ADM) as a substitute. But it is ethanol where the company relies almost totally on federal policy: Companies that use ethanol get a large tax break, and because ADM makes about half the ethanol in the country, it stands to profit handsomely from federal rules mandating ethanol's purchase by consumers (who have been otherwise resistant to the charms of the questionable gas).*

"Why does ADM get these special deals?" asked Stossel. "Bribery. Okay, it's not bribery—that would be illegal. ADM just makes 'contributions.'"[32]

Actually, ADM went well beyond traditional, run-of-the-mill "contributions." Andreas flew politicians on the company's private jets, hosted influential politicians and media types at his lavish Florida retreat, and even arranged for Elizabeth Dole, wife of Senator Bob Dole, then the Senate majority leader, to buy a three-room apartment at a significant discount.

In a profile of Andreas in 1995, *Mother Jones* described the interlocking relationship between ADM and the federal government, noting that "no other U.S. company is so reliant on politicians and governments to butter its bread."[33]

---

* *Mother Jones* detailed the special bennies extended to ADM: Beyond the corn-price support program, the company also benefited from the federal sugar program, which the magazine compared to a mini-OPEC, "setting prices, limiting production, and forcing Americans to spend $1.4 billion per year more for sugar," according to the General Accounting Office. In addition, ADM benefits from ethanol tax credits and subsidies. "Since ADM makes 60 percent of all the ethanol in the country, the government is essentially contributing $2.1 billion to ADM's bottom line. No other subsidy in the federal government's box of goodies is so concentrated in the hands of a single company." (Dan Carney, "Dwayne's World," *Mother Jones*, July/August 1995.)

Confronted about his influence peddling, Andreas is as shameless as any moocher in this book. Stossel recounted this exchange:

Stossel: *Mother Jones* [magazine] pictured you as a pig. You're a pig feeding at the welfare trough.

Andreas: Why should I care?

Stossel: It doesn't bother you?

Andreas: Not a bit.[34]

And why should he be embarrassed? Although he retired in 1999, Andreas was still bringing home the bacon. In October 2010, the Obama administration granted a waiver allowing for a higher blend of ethanol known as E15 to be used in cars, light trucks, and sport utility vehicles, despite questions about its effectiveness, safety, and impact on food prices.[35]

ADM won big. Again.

Chapter 9

THE TWO AMERICAS

During his 2008 presidential run, candidate John Edwards frequently cited what he called the two Americas, a reference to what he saw as the gap between the rich and the poor. But the term applies equally to the gap between average America and the new privileged class of public employees, who enjoy expensive fringe benefits and lavish pensions that increasingly define a growing divide among Americans. Even as private-sector workers struggle to find and keep jobs and pay their bills, politicians have lavished expensive perks on public employees under the baleful eyes of ever more powerful public employee unions. As a result, one America (generally private-sector taxpayers) is now tasked with saving and funding their own retirements, while also paying in to the pensions of public employees, many of whom can retire in their 50s (or even in their 40s), sometimes with six-figure pensions. In California more than fifteen thousand former government workers have pensions that pay them more than $100,000 a year, a number that is growing by 40 percent a year.[1] To match a pension of that size, a private-sector worker would have to accumulate roughly $2.5 million in savings. (More about that later.)

As he wages his own quixotic war against bloated public pensions, New Jersey governor Chris Christie relates the story of one 49-year-old retiree who had paid a total of $124,000 toward his retirement pension and health benefits. "What will we pay him?" asked Christie. "$3.3 million in pension payments and health benefits." A retired teacher who contributed $62,000, says Christie, will get $1.4 million in pension benefits plus $215,000 in health care benefit premiums over her lifetime.[2]

"[There are] two classes of people in New Jersey: public employees who receive rich benefits and those who pay for them," said Christie.[3]

As compelling as the anecdotes of excess are (and there will be many in this chapter), they do not begin to capture the full picture of the public-pension tsunami* bearing down on taxpayers. The unfunded liabilities for bloated state pensions is generally a mystery, but Joshua Rauh, a professor of finance at Northwestern University's Kellogg School, sees deficits of between $3.2 and $5.2 trillion—a massive burden that will inevitably be shifted onto the taxpayers and perhaps lead to a new round of bailouts. Even if they manage to earn a generous return of 8 percent on their investments, Professor Rauh warns that seven states will have run out of money by 2020. By 2027 fully half will have exhausted their pension assets.[4]

How have we gotten here?

During flush times, politicians have also rushed to fatten benefits, with the argument that higher stock prices will pay for the increased pensions and that taxpayers have nothing to worry about. By the time the public is faced with massive unfunded liabilities and escalating contributions, it is often too late to stop the hemor-

---

* There is a Web site by that name: http://www.pensiontsunami.com.

rhaging. When, for example, the California legislators voted to jack up state pensions in 1999, they were told in a brochure from the California Public Employees' Retirement System that the increase wouldn't cost the state any additional money—they were assured that the pension hikes would all be covered by investment earnings. At the same time, the system's own actuaries tried to warn that if the markets did not follow a rose-colored scenario, the cost to the state could explode, from $159 million in 1999 to more than $3.9 billion in 2010–11. As blogger Ed Mendel points out, that forecast "scored a near bulls-eye" on the $3,888 billion state payment for a recent fiscal year.[5] Unfortunately those warnings were ignored, as they were in states and cities across the country.

As fringe benefit and pension costs balloon, government budgets are eaten from within, sucking up money that is no longer available to fund police officers on the street or teachers in the classrooms; increasingly budgets are hostage to ever more costly fringe and retiree benefits.* In New York City, for example, the cost of employee pensions is equal to the budgets for the fire and police departments combined.[6] In California, *The Sacramento Bee* noted that "this year, the city of Roseville will spend as much to fund its pension plan as it does on parks and recreation. San Luis Obispo will spend six times as much on pensions as it does prosecuting criminals." The paper quoted one official as saying, "County government is becoming a pension provider that provides government services on the side."[7]

David Crane, an aide to former California governor Arnold

---

* Steven Greenhut writes: "Pension payments are senior obligations of the state to its employees and accordingly have priority over every other expenditure except Proposition 98 (i.e., K–14) expenditures and arguably even before debt service." David Crane, chief pension adviser to former California governor Arnold Schwarzenegger, notes that they must be funded before other programs: "All of the consequences of rising pension costs fall on the budgets for programs such as higher education, health and human services, parks and recreation and environmental protection that are junior in priority and therefore have their funding reduced whenever more money is needed to pay for pension costs. (Nieman Reports, "How Severe Is the US Pension Crisis," http://www.niemanwatchdog.org/index.cfm?fuseaction=ask_this .view&askthisid=00475.)

Schwarzenegger, put that state's pension tsunami in perspective: "This year [2010] we're spending 10 percent less on higher education than we did 10 years ago, parks and recreation 40 percent less, environmental protection 80 percent less, while spending on pensions is up 2,500 percent."[8]

There are several reasons for this. Government is the most heavily unionized sector in the American economy and the public employee unions have become adept at making their political influence felt at the polls, with the effect of making many of the decision makers actually beholden to the unions with whom they are ostensibly negotiating. Adding to the conflict of interest, many officeholders share in the generous benefits they grant to other public employees. During the 2010 midterm election cycle, for example, the largest public employee union, AFSCME, spent more than $87 million to back Democratic candidates; the union's expenditures amounted to nearly a third of the pro-Democrat independent spending in that year's campaign. The ballooning expenditures—up from just $19 million in 1997–98—reflect both the growing number of government jobs and the higher stakes in preserving unions gains.* "We're the big dog," boasted the head of AFSCME's political operations.[9]

We're All Greeks Now

Americans got a glimpse of their fiscal future when European markets, currencies, and politics were roiled over the impending bank-

---

* In addition to AFSCME, the National Education Association, the nation's biggest teachers' union, dropped $40 million on the campaign. AFSCME's $87.5 million also exceeds the $75 million spent on pro-Republican campaign efforts by the U.S. Chamber of Commerce. (Brody Mullin and John D. McKinnon, "Campaign's Big Spender," *Wall Street Journal*, October 22, 2010.)

ruptcy of some of their profligate nations, most notably Greece, which had made a science of the easy life. Greeks who worked in so-called arduous jobs retired at age 50 for women and 55 for men. More than sixty jobs qualified for the early retirements, including musicians, radio personalities, waiters, and hairdressers.[10] A Greek was even luckier to land a government job. As Michael Lewis reported in *Vanity Fair*:

> In just the past decade the wage bill of the Greek public sector has doubled, in real terms—and that number doesn't take into account the bribes collected by public officials. The average government job pays almost three times the average private-sector job. . . . Twenty years ago a successful businessman turned minister of finance named Stefanos Manos pointed out that it would be cheaper to put all Greece's rail passengers into taxicabs: it's still true.[11]

Columnist Mark Steyn described the attitude that helped create the fiscal disaster: "[In Greece] public sector workers have succeeded in redefining time itself. . . . When they retire, they get 14 monthly pension payments. In other words: Economic reality is not my problem. I want my benefits. And, if it bankrupts the entire state a generation from now, who cares as long as they keep the checks coming until I croak?"[12]

While the specific practices differ, how is that attitude any different from the American public sector? Despite cratering budgets and the prospect of mass teacher layoffs, teachers' unions in Buffalo continued to fight for taxpayer-funded cosmetic surgery, while the union in Milwaukee went to court to get coverage of Viagra.[13] Exploding class sizes? Kids who can't read? Budgets careening toward fiscal black holes? Not my problem . . . *as long as they keep the checks coming until I croak.*

Who's the Public Servant?

And, indeed, government continues to take care of itself quite well:

- Before President Obama announced a two-year freeze on federal pay (which did not freeze actual pay) the number of federal workers making more than $150,000 a year had risen by 1,000 percent in the last decade and, reported *USA Today*, had doubled in the first eighteen months of the Obama presidency.[14] Between December 2007 and June 2009, the number of federal employees making more than $100,000 rose by 46 percent; the number making $150,000 or more rose 119 percent; the number making $170,000 or more rose 93 percent.[15]

- An analysis by *USA Today* found that during a time of stagnating wages and benefits, the total compensation for federal workers—salary plus generous fringe benefits—had grown to twice the average in the private sector. In 2009 the average federal employee's pay and benefits came to $123,049, compared with private workers, whose average pay and benefits were worth $61,051.[16] From 2001 to 2009 average annual private pay grew by 24.9 percent while federal pay grew by 38.4 percent; as a result the gap between the compensation of federal and private-sector workers doubled from $30,415 in 2000 to $61,998 in 2009. Another study found that federal workers were paid more than private-sector workers in more than eight of ten occupational categories.[17]

- A Freedom of Information Act request by the Asbury Park Press found that in 2010, 1.3 million federal workers were handed $408 million in taxpayer-funded bonuses—up $80 million despite the deepest recession in memory.[18]

- The private-public gap has also grown at the state and local level. The average hourly compensation for private-industry employees was $27.42 in hourly salary and benefits in December 2009, lagging far behind the $39.60 per hour in total compensation for state and local government.[19]

The Millionaire Bureaucrat

But the largest gap between the two Americas can be found in the pension system. Let's put this in perspective: The vast majority of private-sector workers no longer have so-called defined pension benefits. Fully half of the nation's private-sector workers have no retirement savings plan and will have to rely on Social Security and whatever savings they manage to set aside after taxes and living expenses. Two-thirds of the remaining 50 percent will rely on 401(k)s to which they must make contributions and possibly also receive a modest employer's match. The value of those accounts plunged from 2007 to 2009 and many workers now find themselves well short of the amount of money they will need to retire. A 2010 study by the Employee Benefit Research Institute found that 47 percent of baby boomers between the ages of 56 and 62 and nearing retirement age do not have enough in savings to avoid running out of money in retirement.[20]

In contrast, public employees like those in Wisconsin may contribute little or nothing while reaping pensions that can replace most of their preretirement income. So while the rest of us try to find a way to save to be able to put aside 10 to 15 percent of our pay every year, state employees face no such pressure. Nor do they have to worry about the stock market like their private counterparts: They can benefit from a rising market, but most are generally insulated from losses by their pension guarantees. As Steve Greenhut notes: "If such 'roll of the dice' investments pay off, then there's more money for public employees and less political pressure to reform the pension system, and if they don't, the taxpayers are on the hook. It's the ultimate privatization of gain and socialization of risk."[21]

Former California governor Schwarzenegger has pointed out the yawning disparities between the two Americas: Between 2007 and 2010, California had lost a million private-sector jobs and retirement accounts of private-sector workers had dropped nearly 20 percent. At the same time, the guaranteed pension benefits of government workers, "for which private sector workers are on the hook," had risen in value. Very few average Californians had $1 million in savings, he noted, "but that's effectively the retirement account they guarantee to public employees who opt to retire at age 55 and are entitled to an annual inflation-protected check of $43,000 for the rest of their lives."[22]

It's actually much worse than that.

In many California cities, police officers and firefighters can retire at the age of 50, with a salary equal to 3 percent of their highest salary times their years of service. So a firefighter in a city like Carlsbad, California, who retires at age 55 after twenty-eight years on the job will receive an annual pension of $76,440 from the city.

What would a private-sector employee have to save to equal that sort of pension?

Forbes publisher Rich Karlgaard crunched the numbers, noting that investment experts suggest drawing no more than 4 percent of retirement savings a year, which is also a reasonable rate of return on conservative investments.

Based on this small but unfortunately realistic 4% return, an $80,000 annual pension payout implies a rather large pot of money behind it—$2 million, to be precise.

That's a lot. One might guess that a $2 million stash would be in the 95th percentile for the 77 million baby boomers who will soon face retirement.

That $2 million also happens to be the implied booty of your average California policeman who retires at age 55.[23]

By the same formula, a $100,000 pension would require private savings of $2.5 million, a $200,000 annual pension requires savings of $5 million, and so on.

Scandals

This taxpayer largesse falls on the worthy and the unworthy alike.

A Buffalo police detective, serving forty-five years in prison, is collecting a $40,544 annual pension; so too is disgraced New York State Comptroller Alan G. Hevesi, who collected a $166,000 pension even after pleading guilty to a felony corruption charge. Not even a conviction for sexually abusing five members of a Boy Scout troop he once led can keep another New York teacher from pulling down his $52,073 annual pension while he sits behind bars.[24] There are other ways to game the system as well: A retired NYC firefighter who received a tax-exempt disability pension for asthma spent his retirement running marathons—and was able to run a six-minute mile—even though his disability included "reduced lung capacity."[25]

The city of Yonkers, New York, has boosted the pensions of police officers by having them work overtime as flagmen on

Consolidated Edison construction sites—then reporting the work as city overtime even though the company was picking up the cost. At least one hundred retired Yonkers cops and firefighters were paid more in pensions than they made in salary before retiring. In one notorious case, a city employee who retired at age 44 with a base salary of $74,000 was reportedly pulling down an annual pension of $101,333.[26]

Perhaps not surprisingly, in a recent study, nineteen of the twenty highest paid city workers in New York State were on Yonkers's payroll.[27] Even though unemployment in the Empire State remained high in 2010, there were ninety-nine thousand state and local workers bringing home six-figure salaries.[28]

The stories (and scandals) are legion:

- In Bell, California, the police chief worked a single year at a salary of $457,000 before retiring with the government pension that will pay him $448,000 a year. This paled next to the city manager's potential $890,000 annual pension.[29]

- In the modest blue-collar suburb of Bellwood, Illinois, a community with a per capita income of $24,000, taxpayers paid city administrator Roy McCampbell $472,000 in 2009, at that time by far the most of any municipal employee in the state. He managed the huge payday despite having a base salary of just $129,000; he was able to pad it by cashing in unused sick and vacation days. Even more creatively, he was paid for performing the duties of ten positions, including comptroller, administrator, public safety CEO, finance director, budget director, human resources director, mayoral assistant, corporation counsel, property commission director, and development corporation officer. When McCampbell retired he became the state's top pensioner, with an annual payout of $250,000.

"I didn't hold a gun to anybody's head to get this," he told the *Chicago Tribune.* "I'm not trying to do anything bad."[30]

- In another Chicago suburb, taxpayers learned they were funding a parks director who was being paid $435,000 a year. Once again, the director's base salary was relatively modest at $164,000, but it was enhanced by $270,000 in bonuses granted by the local parks commission. That conveniently boosted the director's pension to $166,000—which means that he will now make more in retirement than his former base salary. Two other employees also benefited from the commission's spending splurge. Even after the sweet deals were exposed by the *Chicago Tribune,* officials defended their generosity with taxpayer money. "Parks officials in the northern suburb say it was a good use of taxpayer dollars," reported the *Tribune,* "even though the off-the-charts spending spree included giving the three executives nearly $700,000 in bonuses while paying one of them $185,120 for no work and signing over an SUV to him as he left town."

    Ultimately, several parks commissioners were forced to resign, but the retired director will continue to be paid as long as he lives.[31]

- In Governor Christie's state of New Jersey, auditors found the state's Turnpike Authority blew $43 million on "unneeded perks and bonuses." One employee with a base salary of $73,469 actually pulled down $321,985 after a series of payouts and bonuses. Among the various perks for the turnpike employees: $430,000 for free E-ZPass transponders so that employees could get to work. All of the goodies were handed out even as tolls were being raised.[32]

- In Milwaukee, Wisconsin, county officials voted themselves huge pension benefits that included so-called backdrop payments.* Even though the pension scandal sparked a voter revolt that forced the county executive and several supervisors out of office, the pension payouts continue. In 2010, one 66-year-old assistant district attorney retired with a backdrop payment of almost $1.1 million, in addition to an annual pension of $66,024.[33]

Not even the Greeks can sustain that sort of spending for long.

Two Scoops

Public pensions are so generous that many public employees come back for seconds.

Double-dipping from the public trough is fairly widespread, including a Florida college president who pocketed an $893,286 retirement lump-sum payment on top of his $14,631 monthly pension—while still drawing $441,538 in salary.[34] It was all perfectly legal: Florida law allows officials to "retire" for thirty days and then return to work at their old jobs at full salary, while collecting their pensions. The *St. Petersburg Times* found that nearly ten thousand Florida officials collect pensions and paychecks from the public. North Florida County state's attorney Willie Meggs announced that he had "simply changed his mind about plans to retire," a decision that meant he could (1) collect a lump sum of $519,995, (2) his full annual salary of $151,139, and (3) a monthly pension of $7,749. "It's my cotton-picking money," he explained.[35]

---

* Backdrop payments are a creative way of dramatically boosting public-employee pensions. They allow government workers to collect a lump sum equal to the amount of pension they would have received if they had retired on the date they were eligible for retirement up to the day they actually leave their jobs. In Milwaukee, workers hired before 1982 were also given a 25 percent pension bonus. For longtime county employees, this could mean seven-figure payouts.

Well, it is now.

In Phoenix, when the city's police chief Jack Harris retired from his job in 2007, he received a one-time lump sum of $562,000 and began receiving a $90,000 annual city pension. But just two weeks after retiring, the city rehired him with the title Public Safety Manager—a position nearly identical to his old job—at a salary of $193,000 a year.[36]

College presidents also got in on the double-dipping: The president of Indian River State College pocketed more than $585,000 in a lump sum and supplemented his $286,470 salary with a monthly state pension of $9,823. At Northwest Florida State College, the president earned an annual salary of $228,000, which was then supplemented with a monthly pension of $8,803 and a lump-sum payment of $553,228 in 2007.[37]

Florida, unfortunately, was not alone. The retired superintendent of the New Trier Township High School district in Illinois collected a $261,681-per-year pension, but he was able to supplement that generous benefit with a salary of $170,000 as superintendent of a school district in California, putting his combined total compensation at $431,681. Even though Illinois law bars double-dipping, the rule does not apply to officials who cross state lines, and an investigation by the *Chicago Tribune* found that leaving the state "is one of the most lucrative ways for retired superintendents to collect multiple checks."[38]

In Washington State, educational bureaucrats also enjoy the sweet taste of the double-dip at the public trough—without having to move or even change jobs. Consider Greg Royer, a vice president at Washington State University, whose $304,000 annual salary makes him one of the state's highest paid employees. As *The Seattle Times* reported, Royer is one of many employees who supplement their taxpayer-funded salaries with taxpayer-funded pensions. For seven years, Royer collected an annual pension of $105,000 on top of his salary. It is important to note here that Royer did not break

the law, but simply took advantage of the system rigged for employees like him. His double-dip was not especially unusual. The
newspaper found "at least 40 university or community-college employees" took advantage of a loophole that allowed them to retire
and then be rehired within weeks, "often returning to the same job
without the position ever being advertised. That has allowed them
to double dip by collecting both a salary and a pension."[39]

Here's how it worked for Royer: He was first hired on October
1, 1973; on his thirtieth anniversary, October 1, 2003, he "retired."
One month to the day later, on November 1, he was "rehired" and
thus commenced receiving both salary and full pension. As the
paper noted: "Royer, 61, has collected about $700,000 in retire-
ment benefits while continuing to draw his salary. In recent years,
he's been responsible for overseeing some of the deepest budget
cuts in the university's history. Last year, for instance, WSU announced it was cutting about 360 jobs, axing its theater and dance
program and hiking tuition by 14 percent."[40]

Then there was Rick Rutkowski, the president of Green River
Community College, who executed a similar maneuver to fatten his
wallet. Rutkowski, who made $179,000 a year, "retired" on Decem-
ber 1, 2001, was rehired exactly one month later on January 1, and
collected a $64,000 annual pension in addition to his salary. As an
editorial writer for *The Seattle Times* later marveled: "Rutkowski
amazingly does not believe what he did was ethically wrong."

"I had served 30 years and consequently was entitled to the
pension," he told the *Times*. "I don't think there are any ethical issues involved, regardless of the fact that it doesn't feel good for
many people."

No Greek bureaucrat could have put it any better.

As *The Seattle Times* noted, Royer and Rutkowski were hardly
alone. The paper found nearly two thousand double-dipping state
employees at a cost to taxpayers of $85 million a year. This pales in
comparison to Ohio, whose teachers' retirement system paid out

more than $741 million to 15,857 faculty and staff members who were still working for school systems and accumulating a second retirement plan. In Ohio, the average teacher retired at the age of 59.[41]

In North Carolina, the highest paid pensioner in the state was the former director of a mental health program who retired with an annual benefit of $211,373, despite the fact that the state auditor had said his agency "wasn't performing the functions it was supposed to be carrying out and that he was grossly overpaid." Eventually, his operation was shut down and he was rendered redundant. But as a local newspaper reported: "[I]t turns out that he had been doing a very good job of feathering his own nest. He had retired in 2005, and then returned to the same job as a 'contractor' but at the much higher salary of $319,000 a year. Thus, when he 'retired' again, his pension had zoomed from $145,000 (which still seems a gracious plenty) to its present mind-boggling level, making him one of only two state retirees pulling down more than $200,000."[42]

Urban Myths

Many of the perks and benefits for public employees are sustained and supported by the equivalent of urban legends. Foremost among the defenses has been the longstanding and now absurdly out-of-date claim that the generous benefits for public employees compensates for their lower salaries. Now that those salaries eclipse their private counterparts, the justification is inoperative, even among public-employee zealots. More recently, generous fringes and retirements benefits for uniformed employees have been defended on the grounds that police officers and firefighters die young, and so merit the special treatment. This is a compelling political argument, especially after 9/11, and clearly police officers and firefighters are called on to take risks above and beyond most employees in the private sector. But do those risks justify such a dramatic differential? Police and fire services, after all, do not have a monopoly on danger. In fact, according to the Bureau of Labor Statistics, the most dangerous jobs in America are:

1. Commercial fishing jobs
2. Timber logging
3. Aircraft pilots and flight engineers
4. Structural iron and steel workers
5. Farmers and ranchers[43]

Teachers, college administrators, and government bureaucrats do not make the list, and few fishermen or loggers enjoy the sort of retirement and pension perks enjoyed by public-sector pencil pushers.

California's "3 percent at 50" (3 percent of their final year's pay times the number of years worked, available at age 50) pensions for public-safety employees is championed by unions on the grounds that so many cops and firefighters die young. Some union propagandists go so far as to claim that the typical cop or firefighter lasts only five to eight years past retirement. But these claims are not supported by retirement system data. In fact, California's retirement system has found that police and firefighters are, in fact, the longest living categories of public-sector employees. As Steve Greenhut noted, public-safety employees "live on average into the low- to mid-80s." And the high rate of duty disability claims? Greenhut reported that *The Sacramento Bee* once found that "82 percent of manager level officers in the California Highway Patrol retired on disability—a number that spiked after CHP shut down its fraud division."[44]

Working for the Man

What all of this means is that private-sector workers work longer, for less pay, and with fewer benefits to support an increasingly affluent public sector. Americans for Tax Reform found that in 2010, taxpayers now work 231 days out of the year "just to meet all costs imposed by government—8 days later than last year and a full 32 days longer than 2008."[45]

Put another way, government at all levels now consumes more than 63 percent of the national income. Workers have to work 104 days to cover the cost of the federal government; and another 52 days to pay the freight for state and local government; and another 74 days just to cover the cost of complying with the regulations promulgated by government bureaucracies.

It would be unfair to blame all of this on public employees, many of whom work hard at difficult and crucial jobs. The same cannot be said of the public-employee unions and their incestuous nexus with the politicians who have abetted their rise and bloat. The public-union experiment over the last half century has been a disaster: The unions have become an entrenched, obdurate, and grasping special interest devoted to expanding government spending and employment, even at the expense of public services. Ironically, the public-employee unions bear only a passing resemblance to their private counterparts. Government is a monopoly. Unlike private unions, there is no competition that limits their appetites or against which their demands can be measured. Public employees also enjoy civil service protections that are largely unknown in the private sector.

Even in times of economic distress, the unions remain a powerful barrier to reform and innovation, protecting the status quo as they protect their own powers, privileges, and perks no matter how unsustainable. The result is that public employees have become a new class of takers, increasingly mooching off taxpayers even as services are curtailed, especially at the local and state level.

The war in Wisconsin demonstrated just how far they are willing to go to hold on to their claim on other people's money.

The Moocher Empire
Strikes Back

In early 2011, traditionally progressive Wisconsin became ground zero for the fight over public-employee privileges.

When Wisconsin governor Scott Walker proposed curtailing public-employee-union power, the state's capitol was besieged by hundreds of thousands of protestors and gripped by weeks of legislative gridlock and legal wrangling. Teachers staged illegal sickouts, legislators received death threats, businesses were threatened with boycotts, and civil rights leaders descended on Madison, Wisconsin, trailing clouds of apocalyptic rhetoric unheard since the heady days of the sixties. Reverend Jesse Jackson Sr. likened the struggle to preserve union power not only to the civil rights movement, but also to the Exodus, comparing the mild-mannered and somewhat wonkish Walker to "a modern-day Pharaoh."[46] This was relatively benign compared with protestor signs that compared the governor to deposed Egyptian dictator Hosni Mubarak and to Adolf Hitler.

Ironically, the protests had been launched by some of the most generously compensated public employees in the country, who were being asked to make relatively modest contributions to the state's massive deficit. Wisconsin had lost more than 170,000 jobs in the

Great Recession—almost all in the private sector—and the state's per capita income had fallen below the national average. Even so, Wisconsin's overall tax burden continued to be among the heaviest in the nation, in part because government workers had been shielded from the economic tribulations. State employees in Wisconsin, for instance, enjoyed one of the best pension systems in the country. Those pensions were funded by contributions from the state and from the employees themselves—*except that the state also paid the "employee" portion of the pensions.* As a result, while taxpayers contributed $1.37 billion a year into the state's pension fund in 2009, most state employees paid precisely nothing toward their own retirements.

Governor Walker's proposal would have required them to contribute 5.8 percent of their salaries toward those pensions, as well as 12.6 percent of the cost of their increasingly expensive health care premiums. Even with the additional health care costs, government workers would be paying less than half of the national average for health insurance.* Taxpayers had been contributing $1 billion a year on employee health insurance, while Wisconsin's pampered public employees paid a mere $64 million.[47]

The union's dramatic backlash exposed not only the gap between the benefits of the public and private sectors, but also the depth of the sense of entitlement among well-heeled public employees who had drunk deep from the cup of victimism. In some respects, Madison may have represented the first Greece-like moocher rebellion.

---

* Before Walker's proposal, Wisconsin taxpayers were paying $19,128 toward the average employee's family premium. The average employee contributed a mere $936. Under Walker's plan, employee contributions would have averaged about $2,500, still far less than the average private-sector employee's contribution.

Break Out the Violins

Among the many tales of woe that appeared in the media in the wake of the Wisconsin protests was the melancholy tale of two public schoolteachers from Oshkosh, Wisconsin, who put in their retirement papers in the wake of the union reforms.

"Not only am I losing salary and benefits and facing a bigger work load, but now they are taking away my rights," a 56-year-old elementary schoolteacher named Mary Herricks told *The Wall Street Journal*. "Retirement was supposed to be something happy. I'm so sad."[48]

But a quick search of online databases takes some of the edge off the gloom. Ms. Herricks earned a salary of $68,423. The paper noted that even though she was retiring at 56, she would be able to collect "nearly her former salary" in pension benefits. It got better. Her husband, the local head of the teachers' union, was also retiring from a position that paid him $75,916 a year; between the two of them, they made more than $140,000 a year. When generous fringe benefits are added in, the couple earned more than $190,000 in salary and benefits.

Nor would their decision to retire pinch very much at all. Both of them will receive taxpayer-funded health insurance until they turn 65, as well as a payment worth about $600 per year of service, which would amount to about $43,000 on top of their pensions. They will also be able to earn additional income by working as substitute teachers. "Given that pensions are off-limits to certain taxes," noted the *Journal*, "Mr. Herricks says they will bring home close to what they did before." Few, if any, private-sector employees in Wisconsin would be able to say the same.

All About the "Rights"

As the battle over the two Americas escalated in Wisconsin, union leaders executed a tactical pivot, insisting that the uproar was not really about money at all, but rather about "rights." Walker's proposal included sharply curtailing the ability of government unions to bargain for anything other than wages and eliminated both mandatory union membership and the automatic deduction of union dues from public-employee paychecks. Some of the government unions said they would agree to the increased pension and health care contributions, but insisted they be able to retain all of their collective bargaining rights. Protestors claimed that those "rights" to bargain were fundamental civil rights. This was, of course, errant nonsense.

There is no "right" to collective bargaining. Most federal employees are not permitted to collectively bargain either for wages or for benefits—and have never been allowed to do so, under either Republican or Democratic presidents.

In fact, the concept of government unions is of quite recent provenance. No less a giant of progressivism than Franklin Delano Roosevelt had opposed the idea of public-employee unions. "The process of collective bargaining, as usually understood, cannot be transplanted into the public service," wrote FDR. "I want to emphasize my conviction that militant tactics have no place" in the public sector. "[A] strike of public employees manifests nothing less than an intent on their part to obstruct the operations of government until their demands are satisfied. Such action looking toward the paralysis of government by those who have sworn to support it is unthinkable and intolerable." Even labor boss George Meany, the president of the AFL-CIO, turned a doubtful eye on the idea of public-employee unions. "The main function of American trade unions is collective bargaining," he wrote in 1955. "It is impossible to bargain collectively with the government."[49]

Even today, government workers are allowed to collectively bargain in only roughly half the states, while others sharply limit who is allowed to come to the bargaining table. Indiana, Texas, and North Carolina do not permit public-employee bargaining at all.[50] "At last report," quipped columnist Jeff Jacoby, "democracy, fundamental rights, and freedom were doing just fine in all of them."

In practice, collective bargaining is less about rights than about power, as over time governments have ceded more and more authority and benefits to unions. In Madison, for example, in the voluminous teachers' contract, the list of items subject to collective bargaining included everything from the size of bulletin boards to lighting, noise, chairs, footrests, adjustable terminals and keyboards, wall coverings and carpets, and room temperature. Even starting cars during cold weather was subject to collective bargaining. So great was the clout of the teachers' union that they were able to insist that school districts throughout the state make deals with the *union's own insurance company* to purchase health insurance, even though it often cost far more than comparable policies.[51]

After years of collective bargaining and growing union power, state and local government in Wisconsin were rife with stories of bloated salaries and benefits. The highest paid municipal employee in Madison, for example, was a bus driver who pulled down a salary of $159,258 in 2009. That total included more than $109,000 in overtime that he was required to be paid through the union contract. More than a dozen state prison guards also made more than $100,000 in 2009, using generous overtime provisions that their union had negotiated with the state. In a practice known as "sick leave stacking," guards were able to call in sick for one shift, but show up for the next shift and be paid time and a half. As Walker's office later noted, "This results in the officer receiving 2.5 times his or her rate of pay, while still only working 8 hours."*

Riding the collective bargaining gravy train, some Wisconsin teachers were able to get a full year's salary for just thirty days of actual work. In Green Bay, for example, the teachers' union contract created an "emeritus program," under which teachers were paid a full year's salary—in addition to their already generous pension—for showing up just thirty days over a three-year period.[52] Madison's teachers had an even sweeter deal, since they had collectively bargained for an "emeritus program" that paid retirees nearly $10,000 a year on top of their pensions. Unlike the Green Bay deal, Madison teachers were not required to show up for a single day of work to receive the benefit.

In another school district teachers enjoyed a staggering ninety paid sick days a year. Because the school year in Wisconsin was 180 days long, this meant that they could be paid a full year's salary for just ninety days of work.[53] In Milwaukee, the teachers' union was able to get the district to pay health care premiums for retirees, a benefit that in 2016 will cost $4.9 billion, four times the Milwaukee school system's entire current annual budget.[54]

Life's Blood

Ultimately, the ferocity of the union backlash can be explained simply: It was not about rights. It was not even about the bloated salaries and benefits. It was about power and the threat posed to

---

* "In part because of these practices, thirteen correctional officers made more than $100,000 in 2009, despite earning base wages of less than $60,000 per year. The officers received an average of $66,000 in overtime pay for an average annual salary of more than $123,000 with the highest paid receiving $151,181." (Press release, Governor Scott Walker's office, March 7, 2011.)

that power by proposals to end forced union membership and the automatic collection of dues. The power of labor rests increasingly on the power of public-sector unions, and the mother's milk of their power and political influence is their access to millions of dollars of mandatory, government-collected union dues.

For the unions and their political allies there is no threat more dire than the prospect of letting government workers voluntarily choose whether they will fund the union's coffers. In that respect the story of Indiana governor Mitch Daniels is telling. Daniels wasted little time in cutting off the power of the government unions, eliminating their right to collective bargaining on his second day in office.

"On the second day, we discontinued it and I held my breath," Daniels recalled. "And we didn't have a Madison at all. I often say the only two things that happened were, one, we got the freedom to change things in a major way and, two, 95% of the employees, once it was their free choice, quit paying the dues to the union."[55] Since 2005, the number of state employees in Indiana has dropped from 35,000 to 28,700.

When Daniels became governor, 16,408 government workers paid dues to the public-employee unions. Six years later, just 1,490 did.

Part Four

BAILOUT MADNESS

Lessons in Moral Hazard

✳ ✳ ✳

Allard E. Dembe and Leslie I. Boden define *moral hazard* as "the prospect that a party insulated from risk may behave differently from the way they would if they were otherwise fully exposed to that risk. It arises when an individual or institution does not bear the full consequences of its actions, and therefore tends to act less carefully than they otherwise would, leaving a third party to bear the responsibility for the consequences of those actions."[1]

Here are some thought experiments to illustrate the principle:

☐ Why don't you eat cake, ice cream, and steak every night?

☐ Why aren't you driving your dream car? (Which for the sake of this illustration we assume is a Porsche or Maserati.)

☐ Why did you pay your mortgage this month instead of betting it on the ponies?

☐ Why don't you invest your life savings in your brother-in-law's start-up venture?

What if:

☐ What if you ate all the ice cream you wanted and somebody else got fat?

☐ What if you could eat all of the steak you wanted and somebody else's cholesterol exploded?

☐ What if you could buy any car you wanted . . . on credit, and somebody else had to make the payments?

☐ What if your sugar daddy would cover any of your losses at the track? Would that change your attitude toward gambling?

☐ What if the government would foot the bill for any of your losses?

Think of it as the ice cream/cholesterol/hot car/racetrack/loser-in-law Bailout of 2011.

Notice how the shift of consequences also shifts responsibility and influences behavior. If someone else bears the consequences of your choices, all vestiges of restraint may not be eliminated, but they are probably eroded. You'd make very different decisions.

This is moral hazard.

Chapter 10

MORTGAGE MADNESS

The greatest bailout in history began when the financial world realized that betting trillions of dollars on unaffordable mortgages was a bad idea.

Any account of the housing market before the deluge is necessarily a story of near madness: of ever-increasing risk and financial blindness and recklessness, mixed into a toxic stew of greed and arrogance. The early years of the twenty-first century saw a public-private partnership of financial irresponsibility.

Behind the massive housing collapse was the idea that everyone has a right to a house or at least that it would be a public good if housing was widely distributed to groups and individuals who would normally not be able to afford their own home. This was what was meant by "affordability": that the path to home ownership should be eased for people who had no or almost no down payment; that mortgages should be made available to people with shaky credit histories; and that people should be encouraged to buy homes more expensive than their incomes would suggest they could afford. The mechanisms of affordability were many: subprime mortgages; adjustable rate mortgages (ARMs); interest-only mortgages; guarantees by taxpayer-backed Fannie Mae and Freddie Mac for loans with loosened credit standards. If that wasn't sufficient, there were so-called liar loans, and even the classic NINJA mortgage: no income, no job, no assets.

As the bubble grew, the home mortgage itself was turned on its head, transformed from a stable long-term investment and token of financial prudence and planning into a short-term casino game. Where traditional mortgage standards placed a premium on personal responsibility and financial probity, the new rules rewarded fecklessness and encouraged cutting corners.

No down payment? No problem. Not enough income to service the loan? Easily handled with ARMs and interest-only loans. Lousy credit score . . . just sign here. You need to own this house and we need to make it affordable!

All of that took a wrecking ball to the culture of deferral of gratification, of saving, investing, and working to be able to acquire a house as a visible symbol of responsibility. By short-circuiting the process with a rush to spread the housing wealth, politicians and investors alike ignored warning signs, fought off reform attempts, and pushed further into the murkiest waters of high-risk lending.

The result: massive collapse. Irresponsible lenders, speculators, and borrowers took down with them the value of the homes of responsible homeowners and then applied for bailouts. This was mooching on a global scale.

The Securitization Bubble

In 2000, as the new century dawned, interest-only loans accounted for a mere 0.6 percent of new mortgage loans; by 2005, they had grown to 32.6 percent of the total. By 2004, 46 percent of new home loans in dollar value (33 percent in numbers) were adjustable rate mortgages. And in 2005, 43 percent of first-time buyers put no money down at all.[1]

Many of these were sold by lending outfits anxious to write as many mortgages as fast as possible, with the largest possible dollar values, regardless of risk. How did that happen?

The early 2000s saw a boom in both the "securitization" (the resale of mortgages as investments) and the explosion in so-called nondepository mortgage originators who sprang up, writes Barry Ritholz, like "so many mushrooms in cow dung after a summer rain."[2] The new mortgage brokers aggressively hawked affordable and increasingly exotic mortgages designed to get people into homes they otherwise could not afford.

The deals were possible because the mortgages were not held by the loan originators, but were instead quickly off-loaded. They were abetted by both the federally backed Fannie Mae and Freddie Mac, which bought many of the dicey loans, and by Wall Street, which developed an avaricious craving for more mortgages to slice, bundle, and sell as securities. Wall Street, recalls economics writer Arnold Kling, "made riskier and riskier bets, but as long as home prices kept increasing, defaults were rare and market participants enjoyed nice profits."[3]

In the days before the affordability bubble, it was understood that traditional borrowers would put down large down payments (preferably 20 percent), had good income and credit histories, and could service the mortgage debt easily. These were the so-called prime borrowers and they were prudent bets for lenders. They were also thirty-year deals, so the focus was always on the long-term stability of the lender-borrower relationship. That all changed in the brave new world in which salesmen, paid on the volume of mortgages they could sell, quickly sold them off to whatever greater fool would have them. In other words, notes Ritholtz, the industry underwent an "enormous paradigm shift." Volume—and the pressure to make the sale—replaced prudence, which led to a "radical change in lending standards." Lenders no longer needed to find buyers who would be a good risk for thirty years; "they needed only to find someone who wouldn't default before the securitization process was completed," or about ninety days.[4]

The clamor for the exotic and lucrative mortgages meant that numbers were fudged and standards were bent—incomes were invented or inflated, appraisals massaged, piggy bank loans juggled, value-to-loan ratios ignored, and the money flowed. "If you could fog a mirror, you qualified for a mortgage," quips Ritholtz, noting that a strawberry picker with an annual income of $14,000 was deemed qualified for a mortgage to buy a $720,000 home.[5]

Let's consider that strawberry picker and his $720,000 house for a moment. On one level, the loan was pure madness, but on another, it represented the triumph of the "affordability" crusade. A man making $14,000 a year was able to afford a house valued at three quarters of a million dollars. What could be more affordable than that? Of course, this required a great deal of Other People's Money, but that was always implied in the whole frenzy.

Some of these loans were undoubtedly what could be described as "predatory" (although it is a strange form of predation in which money is pressed on the victim rather than taken from him)— written by unscrupulous lenders anxious to score quick fees and the long-term risks be damned. But even if this is true, there was also predatory *borrowing*, as homeowners leveraged massive increases in their square footage and financed their lifestyles with meager investments of their own money.

Meanwhile the mortgage securities—known as collateralized debt obligations or CDOs—seemed to be paying off handsomely. High ratings and decreasing transparency created the illusion of safety and prudence. Even though many of the mortgages were based on hinky subprime loans, ratings agencies gave them stellar AAA ratings and investors across the globe snapped them up. They became so popular that Wall Street created ultra-exotic CDOs that were backed by other CDOs, each step more complex and less transparent. In other words, nobody really understood what they had or how chancy the whole scheme had become.

All that was left to complete this abdication of common sense was the support of the federal government. Support? The feds were cheerleading the process and bankrolling the march of folly.

As mortgage madness spread, the federal government actively stoked the flames. Far from reining in the spread of questionable loans, Washington pressured Fannie and Freddie to buy increasingly risky loans. "Once," reported *The New York Times,* "a high-ranking Democrat telephoned executives and screamed at them to purchase more loans from low-income borrowers, according to a Congressional source." At the same time, "Shareholders attacked the executives for missing profitable opportunities by being too cautious."[6]

The CEOs of the two federally backed companies "eventually yielded to those pressures, effectively wagering that if things got too bad, the government would bail them out."[7]

This is where moral hazard goes to die.

Bipartisan Madness

While greed undoubtedly drove much of the mortgage mess, politics constantly provided the spur. History will record that the mortgage madness and subsequent bailouts occurred under both Democratic and Republican presidents and that many of the policies and practices that led to the crisis were advanced by both conservatives and progressives (albeit with different motives and agendas).

Even amid warnings that many of the subprime loans were unsustainable, the Bush administration ratcheted up the pressure for riskier loans, in pursuit of what Bush called the "ownership society." Reported *The Washington Post*: "Eager to put more low-income and minority families into their own homes, [the Department of Housing and Urban Development] required that two government-chartered mortgage finance firms purchase far more 'affordable' loans made to these borrowers. Administration officials publicly complained that Fannie and Freddie were not being as aggressive as the private market and must do more."[8] Bush's goal was to create 10 million new homeowners, largely backed by low-interest loans and the implicit government guarantees. To make that possible, Bush's Department of Housing and Urban Development let Fannie and Freddie count the billions of dollars vanishing down the subprime hole as "a public good that would foster affordable housing."[9]

In 2003, Fannie and Freddie bought $81 billion in subprime securities; the next year, they had purchased $175 billion, fully 44 percent of the market. By 2006, Fannie and Freddie had backed off a bit, buying only $90 billion in subprime securities. But the damage had been done: From 2004 to 2006, Fannie and Freddie bought $434 billion in securities backed by subprime loans, fueling the lending frenzy by creating a huge taxpayer-backed market for the funny money loans.[10] "Every dollar they pumped into subprime securities made the real estate bubble worse," declared the conservative Heritage Foundation.[11]

Even as the market began to unravel, Freddie's defenders rationalized the failures. "It's like a kid who gets straight A's and then gets a DUI. Is the kid [messed] up?" one lobbyist for Freddie argued. "No, he made a mistake. . . . You can't just get rid of Fannie and Freddie."[12]

By this point, though, the support for the risky lending was solidly bipartisan.

Laying the Fire

Long before there were subprime, no-down-payment, interest-only mortgages, before the rise of collateralized debt obligations and NINJA mortgages, there was the Community Reinvestment Act, a Carter-era law given teeth under President Bill Clinton. The law was originally designed to encourage banks to make loans in "disadvantaged" neighborhoods. While its role in the housing meltdown has been both downplayed and exaggerated by partisans, the CRA clearly laid the ground for much of what was to follow, including the underlying push for "affordability," the political mantra that drove and rationalized the flight from financial sanity that eventually resulted in the housing crash.

Defenders of the Community Reinvestment Act frequently cite a study from Harvard's Joint Center for Housing Studies that concluded that loans covered by the CRA accounted for just 9 percent of the mortgages given to low-income individuals and neighborhoods. In contrast, independent mortgage companies accounted for the majority of such loans.[13] But this understates the groundbreaking significance of CRA. While Fannie and Freddie and

Wall Street recklessness provided the blowtorch that set off the bonfire, it was the CRA that laid the kindling.

Hindsight, of course, is convenient in the wake of the bursting of a bubble, but there were warnings before the deluge gathered force. In 2000, Howard Husock, writing in *City Journal,* sounded the alarm for what he called "The Trillion-Dollar Bank Shakedown That Bodes Ill for Cities," and explained how the CRA changed the political and financial dynamics of mortgage lending.[14]

For the first decade or so of its regulatory life, Husock noted, the CRA was generally ineffectual. But in the 1990s, the Clinton administration transformed it into "one of the most powerful mandates" shaping the nation's financial system.

Under Clinton, new CRA regulations gave advocacy groups greater clout in pressuring banks to make marginal loans. The new rules required bank regulators to evaluate how well banks responded to such pressure. "The old CRA evaluation process had allowed advocacy groups a chance to express their views on individual banks, and publicly available data on the lending patterns of individual banks allowed activist groups to target institutions considered vulnerable to protest," wrote Husock. But the Clinton administration's formal invitation was a "clarion call" for activists like the National Community Reinvestment Coalition and community groups to mobilize to pressure banks to make more low-income loans.

The impact was swiftly felt. Merely by threatening to complain, activist groups were able to "gain control over eye-popping pools of bank capital, which they in turn parcel out to individual low-income mortgage seekers," observed Husock. Notably, the now-notorious activist group ACORN Housing snagged a $760 million commitment from the Bank of New York. Another group, the Neighborhood Assistance Corporation of America, scored a $3 billion agreement with the Bank of America, and on and on it went, with similar deals in virtually every major city. Husock quoted one "affordable housing" activist who had landed $220 million in mortgage cash to parcel out saying: "CRA is the backbone of everything we do."[15]

Clinton also subtly shifted the focus of the law from poor neighborhoods to low-income individuals, significantly expanding its mandate and ultimately its effect on lending. For Husock, however, the new culture was personified by one activist in particular: Bruce Marks, the CEO of the Neighborhood Assistance Corporation of America. "Bruce Marks has set out to become the Wal-Mart of home mortgages for lower-income households," wrote Husock, with offices in twenty-one states, an annual budget of more than $10 million, and delegated underwriting authority from banks. A self-described "bank terrorist," Marks openly recruited homeowners as activists for his political agenda.

Years before the housing meltdown, Husock predicted that activists like Marks "may well reshape urban and suburban neighborhoods," because they pushed the envelope on the sorts of loans they issued. Because Marks believed that low-income borrowers were oppressed, disadvantaged victims, he regarded requiring down payments from low-income minority buyers as "patronizing and almost racist.'"[16]

An Open Checkbook

So the political stars were aligned for a transformation of the home mortgage industry. Even before the Bush-era "ownership society," Democrat Bill Clinton pushed to expand the number of Americans who owned homes, and the CRA and Fannie and Freddie were key weapons in the battle. In 1995 the Clinton administration gave a green light to Fannie and Freddie to start buying subprime securities, including those backed by mortgages given to low-income borrowers. By 1996 the feds required that fully 40 percent of the loans backed by Fannie and Freddie had to come from buyers with "below median incomes."[17]

"We began to stress homeownership as an explicit goal for this period of American history," Henry Cisneros, then Secretary of Housing and Urban Development, later told *The Washington Post*. "Fannie and Freddie became part of that equation." Noted the *Post*: "The result was a period of unrestrained growth for the companies. . . . The companies increasingly were seen as the engine of the housing boom. They were increasingly impervious to calls for even modest reforms."[18]

Critics lacked the clout to restrain the mortgage giants or their rush to financial recklessness. Defenders like Congressman Barney Frank insisted that the companies with their virtually limitless checkbook served a public purpose because they made mortgages cheaper.[19]

Fannie and Freddie effectively wrapped themselves in the cloak of homeownership, which was recast as an indispensable part of the American Dream, as indeed it was. But a key distinction was overlooked: The *opportunity* to one day own a home was a far cry from a mad rush to provide everyone—even those who couldn't afford one—the means to purchase a sprawling suburban ranch *right now*. Once seen as the end result of a series of choices, sacrifices, and prudent decisions, homeowners now had to be instantly gratified. Artificially cheap loans were what economists call "signal noise," distorting the market and blinding politicians and investors alike to the peril of the expansion of the unaffordable loans.

As long as the music played—and the housing market continued to go up—the game worked: Homeowners got their bigger homes; the originators got their fees; Wall Street was able to reap fat yields; and taxpayers were assured they would never have to pay a nickel for any of this. Fannie and Freddie lubricated friendly politicians with generous campaign donations and kept fueling the subprime market even after it was caught cooking its own books. But when the music did, in fact, stop, the realization set in that the housing bubble had been fueled by funny money and that the dubious mortgages had been quickly shuffled from one hand to another, like a stick of dynamite with a slowly burning wick.

In September 2008, the federal government seized control of Fannie and Freddie and the taxpayer bailouts could amount to hundreds of billions of dollars.* The total price tag for bailing out the financial system could run into the trillions of dollars.

---

* On Christmas Eve 2009, the Treasury Department quietly removed the $400 billion cap on the amount of money taxpayers might have to spend bailing out the profligate Fannie and Freddie. (*Wall Street Journal*, "Fannie and Freddie Amnesia," April 20, 2010.)

Chapter 11

BAILOUTS FOR IDIOTS (HOW TO MAKE OUT BIG BY SCREWING UP)

The Great Bailout of 2008–09 can be summed up simply:

Never have so few mooched so much off so many.*

The numbers are mind-bending—tens of billions of dollars for badly run car companies; hundreds of billions for reckless financiers; trillions to bail out the mortgage insanity of the previous decade. Spurred by dire warnings of financial Armageddon, the bailouts rewrote the rules of finance, exemplified crony capitalism, and transformed the landscape of the free market. Losing large amounts of money is the essence of market discipline; the prospect of failure is precisely what deters businesses from running imprudent risks. But in the Great Bailout the laws of financial gravity

---

* With apologies to Winston Churchill.

were suspended, if not repealed: Some well-connected companies were protected from their losses by the generosity of taxpayers, many of whom were watching their life savings devastated by the financial turmoil.

As shocking as the bailouts seemed at the time, history is likely to be far less kind. The Congressional Oversight Panel's review of the bailout of supermoocher AIG is a withering critique of cronyism, conflicts of interest, favoritism, and profligacy.

> The government's actions in rescuing AIG continue to have a poisonous effect on the marketplace. By providing a complete rescue that called for no shared sacrifice among AIG's creditors, the Federal Reserve and Treasury fundamentally changed the relationship between the government and the country's most sophisticated financial players. . . . Even more significantly, markets have interpreted the government's willingness to rescue AIG as a sign of a broader implicit guarantee of "too big to fail" firms. That is, the AIG rescue demonstrated that Treasury and the Federal Reserve would commit taxpayers to pay any price and bear any burden to prevent the collapse of America's largest financial institutions, and to assure repayment to the creditors doing business with them. So long as this remains the case, the worst effects of AIG's rescue on the marketplace will linger.[1]

Even though taxpayers will recoup some of the original cost of the bailouts, the consequences as well as the costs will be paid not over years, but over generations.

Bailouts, like corporate welfare, are not new. The federal government bailed out Chrysler in 1980, the S&Ls in the 1990s, Penn Central in 1974, and Lockheed in 1971. The Lockheed bailout set a precedent, but even so, that taxpayer rescue cost a mere

$250 million, a small fraction of the money laid out to save Wall Street firms like Bear Stearns, Goldman Sachs, Citigroup, and AIG from their own excesses.

Beginning with the rescue of Bear Stearns for $29 billion, the $700 billion Troubled Asset Relief Program (TARP), the takeover of Fannie Mae and Freddie Mac (which put taxpayers on the hook for $5.5 trillion in debt), the loan guarantees for Citigroup and injection of cash into Bank of America, the $182 billion rescue of insurance giant AIG, and the tens of billions of dollars for Chrysler and General Motors, the bailouts marked a massive transfer of wealth from productive America to a new class of supermoochers.

As details have emerged, questions have multiplied: Were the bailouts really necessary? Were there alternatives to government takeovers? And was there any pattern to the winners and losers? The randomness of the bailouts is perhaps the most puzzling. Bear Stearns was rescued; Lehman Brothers was allowed to die; Citigroup got a stunningly generous bailout. Referring to Citi's sweet deal, author Barry Ritholtz in *Bailout Nation* wrote: "One might assume the government would cut a hard bargain with the biggest, stupidest, most irresponsible bank in the country. . . . Instead, the Treasury essentially handed over the keys to the kingdom for a mere song."[2] By guaranteeing nearly $250 billion in toxic assets, "the liabilities for a full decade of terrible decision making were transferred from Citi's bond-shareholders to the taxpayers—a terrible deal for Uncle Sam, but a fantastic score for Citi."*

The taxpayers were essentially required to underwrite a decade of recklessness made possible by a mad fever of Wall Street greed abetted by misguided deregulation. A caveat here: On balance I support freeing markets from unnecessary rules, mandates, and forest-killing make-work regulations. But some libertarians (and I use

---

* Ritholtz also noted that while other portfolios had been forced to take "haircuts" of 40, 50, even 65 percent, Citi was asked to "suffer only an 11 percent haircut."

this word respectfully) took a Panglossian attitude that sound ethics and prudent common sense would prevent the worst abuses if the government simply got out of the way. As it turned out, they were naïve in assuming that "deregulation" itself would make markets more efficient. As Richard Posner and others have noted, it is one thing to ease the burden of dysfunctional overregulation; it is quite another to use it as a cover for Wall Street to invent bogus new securities that were so lacking in transparency and so fragilely connected to reality that they bordered on the fraudulent. "If you're worried that lions are eating too many zebras, you don't say to the lions, 'You're eating too many zebras,'" said Posner. "You have to build a fence around the lions. They're not going to build it."[3]

Regulators, including Congress, not only failed to build the fences, but they turned out to be as clueless as many of the investors who bought the exotic and highly leveraged securities. The country's biggest firms simply poured fuel on the conflagration.

Casino

In 2004 the Securities and Exchange Commission waived its leverage rules that had limited firms to a maximum debt-capital ratio of 12 to 1. The exemption freed five firms—Goldman Sachs, Bear Stearns, Merrill Lynch, Lehman Brothers, and Morgan Stanley—to leverage their bets up as high as 30 or even 40 to 1.

These were casino-like wagers that would be considered certifiably insane, except for the belief that the value of real estate would continue to rise, as the banks apparently assumed. Here's a simplified version (offered for demonstration purposes only) of the power and perils of leverage at this altitude: At a ratio of 40 to 1, a firm could buy $100 worth of subprime mortgages, for example, with just $2.50 of its own money. Here's the upside: If the value of the investment rose by 5 percent to $105, the firm makes $5 on an investment of just $2.50—a profit of 100 percent, minus any interest payments. Brilliant.

Here's the downside: If our investment of $100 drops in value by 5 percent, it will be worth only $95—and the $2.50 cash investment is transformed into a $5 loss—a loss twice the original investment. If the value drops by 10 percent, the loss becomes four times the original investment. Multiply these numbers by billions of dollars and you realize the panic that began to sweep through Wall Street's high-flying casinos in 2007 and 2008.

As the Great Bailout began, the pattern of determining winners and losers shifted from the roulette wheel of the housing market to the halls of government. But the randomness remained: Some lenders were pressured by the feds to make concessions and take losses on their risky bets in exchange for bailouts; others were paid 100 cents on the dollar with taxpayer cash. But while there was no consistency, there were some discernible patterns. Foremost among them: It's good to be Goldman Sachs.

Government Sachs

Before the Fall, American International Group (AIG) was a AAA-rated monolith with $1 trillion in assets, boasting 76 million customers around the globe. But it became the symbol of the reckless exuberance of the mortgage bubble. Among its many products, AIG's soon-to-be notorious Financial Products subsidiary peddled insurance policies for exotic financial instruments that fueled the explosion of subprime lending. The insurance policies, known as credit default swaps or CDS, underwrote much of the wheeling and dealing of firms like Goldman Sachs. By late 2008 AIG was on the hook for more than $2.7 trillion worth of swap contracts. The swaps were such sure things, the company boasted, that its computers predicted that the odds of never having to pay out any money on the credit swaps was 99.85 percent.[4] AIG's Financial Products unit believed that the CDS were so ironclad that the entire economy would have to descend into a full-scale meltdown before the company would have to pay out a penny to cover the defaulting bonds. As it turned out, billions of dollars in those swaps were held by Goldman Sachs.

Even in an era of crony capitalism, Goldman Sachs stands out. "Goldman, more than any other company," wrote journalist Timothy P. Carney, "pulls the levers of government."[5]

Both the Bush and Obama administrations were packed with Goldman Sachs alumni; and the revolving door between government and the firm became so well established that Goldman won the moniker "Government Sachs." So incestuous was the relationship between Goldman's insiders and the government that the firm was able to orchestrate the Great Bailout to its maximum advantage. At key moments, the interlocking interests blurred distinctions between what was good for Goldman and what was good for everyone else.

For years, Goldman had packaged and marketed subprime mortgages to its clients, but more recently it had reversed its position, actively betting against the housing market by buying credit default swaps that would pay off if the housing bubble burst. Goldman was counting on AIG to pay it billions of dollars if, as it expected, the housing market began to implode. In any case, AIG and its sure-thing credit swaps were crucial for Goldman's bottom line. As *The New York Times* later noted, "Without the insurer to provide credit insurance, the investment bank could not have generated some of its enormous profits betting against the mortgage market. And when that market went south, AIG became its biggest casualty—and Goldman became one of its biggest beneficiaries."[6]

At every step of the AIG bailout, Goldman was at the table. Actually all around the table. A *New York* magazine article captured a key behind-the-scenes moment from 2008:

> At the meeting, it was hard to discern where concerns over AIG's collapse ended and concern for Goldman Sachs began: Among the 40 or so people in attendance, Goldman Sachs was on every side of the large conference table, with "triple" the number of representatives as other banks, says another person who was there. . . .
>
> On the government side, Goldman was also well represented: [Then New York Fed President Timothy] Geithner himself had never worked for Goldman, but he was an acolyte of former Goldman co-chairman and Clinton Treasury secretary Robert Rubin. Former Goldman vice-president Dan Jester served as [Treasury Secretary Henry] Paulson's representative from the Treasury. And though Paulson himself wasn't present, he didn't need to be: He was intimately aware of Goldman's historical relationship with AIG, since the original AIG swaps were acquired on his watch at Goldman.[7]

The meeting was ostensibly to determine whether a private or a combination private-public solution could be found to save the insurance giant, which had insured many of the dicier financial instruments of the housing bubble era. But under the watchful eyes of Goldman, those alternatives collapsed, and days later Paulson announced plans for a complete government bailout—$85 billion in taxpayer money to buy a majority share of the company. As the Congressional Oversight Committee later found: "In previous rescue efforts, the federal government had placed a high priority on avoiding direct taxpayer liability for the rescue of private businesses. . . . With AIG, the Federal Reserve and Treasury broke new ground.

They put U.S. taxpayers on the line for the full cost and the full risk of rescuing a failing company."[8]

Most of that cash went to pay AIG's "counterparties," the largest of whom turned out to be Goldman Sachs itself, which pocketed $13 billion.

That $13 billion represented 100 percent—every last nickel—of what it was owed by AIG. This was extraordinary, noted Joe Hagan in *New York* magazine: Other banks, including Merrill Lynch, had taken much harsher haircuts. "Over time, it would appear to many that Goldman Sachs had received a backdoor bailout from a Treasury Department run by the firm's former CEO."[9]

Goldman later insisted that it was fully protected from any losses from AIG, but the argument is implausible, considering the dire effect that AIG's collapse would have had on Goldman's liquidity and stock price. This, however, raises an intriguing question: "So why did Goldman, supposedly brilliant, expose itself so much to AIG?" asks Timothy Carney. "It's reasonable, given the company's closeness to government to conclude Goldman was counting on a bailout if things went badly."[10] As it turned out, that was a very good bet.

If You're Goldman Sachs, You're Fine. If You're Not, You're %$*&^#

As congressional investigators reconstructed the frenzied bailout process, they were frankly stunned by what they found: the shoddy logic behind the defenses for the raid on the Treasury; the flagrant conflicts of interest; the damage to the marketplace caused by the bailouts; and the sleight of hand used to protect Goldman Sachs. Increasingly it became obvious that the concern behind the bailouts was not to save the system, but rather to rescue certain banks, certain politically well-connected banks. Most egregious of all was the fact that the Goldman-dominated Treasury Department appeared to reject any options for bailing out AIG that did not involve paying the banks 100 cents on the dollar. As *The New York Times* later noted: "All of this was quite different from the tack the government took in the Chrysler bailout. In that matter, the government told banks they could take losses on their loans or simply own a bankrupt company; the banks took their losses."[11] Goldman Sachs was insulated from deep losses, in part because of the extraordinarily cozy relationship with the regulators.

Documents released later by congressional investigators portray officials of the New York Fed truckling to bankers at the very time they were rescuing them from the consequences of their own blunders. "While Wall Street deal-making is famously hard-nosed with participants fighting for every penny," noted *The New York Times*, "during the AIG bailout regulators negotiated in an *almost concilia-tory fashion*."[12] (Emphasis added.)

Congressional investigators were struck by the outrageousness of the conflicts of interest that led to the transfer of billions of dollars from the taxpayers to Goldman Sachs. As the Congressional Oversight Committee later wrote:

> Throughout its rescue of AIG, the government failed to address perceived conflicts of interest. People from the same small group of law firms, investment banks, and regulators appeared in the AIG saga in many roles, sometimes representing conflicting interests. The lawyers who represented banks trying to put together a rescue package for AIG became the lawyers to the Federal Reserve, shifting sides within a matter of minutes. Those same banks appeared first as advisors, then potential rescuers, then as counterparties to several different kinds of agreements with AIG,

and ultimately as the direct and indirect beneficiaries of the
government rescue. The composition of this tightly inter-
twined group meant that everyone involved in AIG's rescue
had the perspective of either a banker or a banking regulator. These entanglements created the perception that the
government was quietly helping banking insiders at the
expense of accountability and transparency.[13]

In other words, the elite negotiated with the elite, for the benefit of the elite and at the expense of the rest of us. Forget the welfare
queens of yore; no one can mooch with quite the élan or grasping
of the rich and powerful.

For example: Treasury's "point man" on the AIG bailout, Daniel
Jester, was a former Goldman executive who still owned Goldman
stock, even as he was negotiating the terms of the bailout. Reported
the *Times*: "According to the documents, Mr. Jester opposed bailout
structures that required the banks to return cash to A.I.G. Nothing
in the documents indicates that Mr. Jester advocated forcing Goldman and the other banks to accept a discount on the deals."[14] As
oversight committee member J. Mark McWatters later observed:

> It is ironic that although the bailout of AIG may have also
> rescued many of its counterparties, none of these institu-
> tions were willing to share the pain of the bailout with the
> taxpayers and accept a discount to par upon the termination
> of their contractual arrangements with AIG. Instead, they
> left the American taxpayers with the full burden of the
> bailout. It is likewise intriguing that these too-big-to-fail
> financial institutions (leading members of the "global
> financial system") were paid at par—that is, 100 cents on
> the dollar—at the same time the average American's 401(k)
> and IRA accounts were in free-fall, unemployment rates
> were sky-rocketing and home values were plummeting.[15]

The Fed documents suggest that Fed officials were sensitive to this disparity and nervous that making firms like Goldman completely whole would look like a "gift." In November 2008, staffers advised keeping that aspect of the deal secret. For more than a year, the Fed successfully blacked out the scope of its concessions to the lucky bankers.

One of the greatest mooches of all time was orchestrated behind closed doors, without transparency, by insiders who were more interested in scratching one another's backs than protecting either the taxpayers or the integrity of the financial system they were supposedly saving.

How Awful?

The rationalizations for the bailout have not stood up well under scrutiny. The Congressional Oversight Committee rejected arguments that the Fed faced a choice of either letting AIG collapse or bailing it out completely with taxpayer funds. The government could have made more efforts to obtain private backing, the committee argued, but instead undertook a deeply flawed effort to put the private rescue in the hands of just two banks, J. P. Morgan and Goldman Sachs, "institutions that had severe conflicts of interest as they would have been among the largest beneficiaries of a taxpayer rescue." When that effort predictably failed, "the Federal Reserve decided not to press major lenders to participate in a private deal or to propose a rescue that combined public and private funds. In short, the government chose not to exercise its substantial negotiating leverage to protect taxpayers or to maintain basic market discipline."[16]

At the heart of AIG's collapse was the usual toxic stew of

irresponsible betting, excessive leveraging, incompetent risk management, incentives that encouraged recklessness, and creative accounting. By bailing out AIG, congressional investigators found, the government distorted the marketplace "by transforming highly risky derivative bets into fully guaranteed payment obligations."

Concluded the Congressional Oversight Committee:

> In the ordinary course of business, the costs of AIG's inability to meet its derivative obligations would have been borne entirely by AIG's shareholders and creditors under the well-established rules of bankruptcy. But rather than sharing the pain among AIG's creditors—an outcome that would have maintained the market discipline associated with credit risks—the government instead shifted those costs in full onto taxpayers out of a belief that demanding sacrifice from creditors would have destabilized the markets. The result was that the government backed up the entire derivatives market, as if these trades deserved the same taxpayer backstop as savings deposits and checking accounts.[17]

As a result, the banks who were owed money on their risky bets got "a complete rescue at taxpayer expense," as did "sophisticated investors who had profited handsomely from playing a risky game and who had no reason to expect that they would be paid in full in the event of AIG's failure."[18]

The political fallout has been dramatic and apparently surprising for the various ruling classes. But the backlash should not have been unexpected either in its intensity or scope; both major parties were complicit in the orgy of bailouts and the mooching of potentially trillions of dollars from taxpayers. The unprecedented transfer of wealth from those who played by the rules to those who screwed up exposed a permanent bipartisan governing class of insiders and elites: Republican Henry Paulson, followed by Democrat

Timothy Geithner, the hapless New York Fed president, who was rewarded for his role in the rescue of improvident billionaire corporations by being named Treasury secretary by President Obama, despite his failure to pay income taxes usually required of the little people whose money he was now charged with managing and whose own taxes he would henceforth be collecting. Bush appointee Ben Bernanke, who orchestrated the bailouts, was similarly reappointed by Obama to head the Federal Reserve, where he continued to conjure dollars from thin air and his own imagination. This perhaps explains why the Tea Party seemed to rise up against insiders in both parties and seemed so intolerant of any hint that it was time to return to business as usual.

Epilogue

On July 15, 2009, *The New York Times* reported that, flush with bailout cash, Goldman Sachs was once more enjoying eye-popping profits:

> Goldman posted the richest quarterly profit in its 140-year history and, to the envy of its rivals, announced that it had earmarked $11.4 billion so far this year to compensate its workers.
>
> At that rate, Goldman employees could, on average, earn roughly $770,000 each this year—or nearly what they did at the height of the boom.[19]

Chapter 12

WALK AWAY FROM YOUR MORTGAGE!

If Moocher Nation had the equivalent of a prom king and queen, they could well be a couple named Alex Pemberton and Susan Reboyras. Thanks to *The New York Times*, they became the public face of a new phenomenon known as strategic default, in which homeowners choose to walk away from their mortgages.*

Far from being seen as a failure, the *Times* reported, Pemberton and Reboyras were among the growing number of defaulters who had embraced foreclosure as "a way of life."[1]

---

* An example of a strategic default would be someone who has taken out a $300,000 mortgage to buy a $380,000 house. If the value of the house drops to, say, $250,000, the mortgagee is considered "underwater," even if they have the income to continue to make monthly payments. Most mortgagees will continue to make those payments, hoping that the value of their home recovers or because they think they have a moral obligation not to walk away. But in strategic default, the homeowner decides to walk away from the mortgage, despite being able to pay for it. A 2009 study found that 26 percent of defaults were strategic.

While policymakers and banks wrestled with bailouts and other forms of mortgage relief, reported the *Times*, Pemberton and Reboyras fashioned "a sort of homemade mortgage modification, one that brings their payments all the way down to zero." Their "mortgage modification" involved simply ceasing to make the $1,837-a-month payment on their mortgage. (Their "plan" is reminiscent of the old Steve Martin joke about how to make a million dollars and pay no taxes. First you make a million dollars, and then pay no taxes. And when the IRS agent comes to your door, you explain, "I forgot.")

Like other strategic defaulters who "are refusing to slink away in shame," the *Times* said the couple regarded foreclosure as "a blessing." They were utterly post-stigma. "Foreclosure has allowed them to stabilize the family business," explained the *Times*. "Go to Outback occasionally for a steak. Take their gas-guzzling airboat out for the weekend. Visit the Hard Rock Casino."[2]

But the couple's nonpayment of their mortgage had an additional wrinkle: They also refused to leave their house. *The Times* explained: "This type of modification does not beg for a lender's permission but is delivered as an ultimatum: Force me out if you can."

Like thousands of others, Pemberton and Reboyras have figured out how to use the law and the system to prolong their squatting. They hired a lawyer who works to stretch the time between default and eviction; in Florida the average house is in foreclosure for more than five hundred days. The *Times* noted that their lawyer sends out thousands of letters to homeowners in foreclosure, assuring defaulters that even if they have no defense, "you may be able to keep living in your home for weeks, months or even years without paying your mortgage." In other words, he was offering Guilt-Free, Perfectly Legal Squatting.

The couple rationalized their mooching by blaming the banks. "Any moral qualms," explains the *Times*, "are overshadowed by a conviction that the banks created the crisis by snookering homeowners with loans that got them in over their heads."

Pemberton and Reboyras fit the profile for many homeowners

who are underwater on their mortgages. According to the *Times*, at the time they stopped paying, they owed about $280,000 on a house worth less than half that amount. But their debt problem was only partly owing to the real-estate crash. The couple ran a business that restored attics infested by rodents or other pests and at one point used their house as an ATM to fund their business, "taking out cash to buy a truck they used as a contest prize for their hired animal trappers."

Even after the crash and their default, they have no regrets about their choice to frivolously run up their debt. In fact, they blame the bank: Pemberton called the bank's decision to loan him the money a "stupid move." Recall that they took out a loan on their home to buy a truck. Not for their own use, but as a "prize."

"They went outside their own guidelines on debt to income," Pemberton explained to the *Times*. "And when they did, they put themselves in jeopardy." Especially when the couple decided that they had no intention of repaying the loan. Instead, the couple decided to take the money they paid for their mortgage and apply it to their business, by buying "print ads, then local television." And, since they were now living rent free, they also had cash left over for the trips to the Hard Rock Casino and steak dinners out.*

It was all quite wonderful, explained Pemberton. Instead of being a weighty and costly obligation, their house had become "a life raft."†

---

* Pemberton and Reboyras later took issue with the *Times's* portrayal, insisting that they only rarely went out on their yellow airboat or visited Outback or casinos. But they continued to defend their decision. In an interview with the *St. Petersburg Times*, they insisted that they were "actually helping the economy by using money saved on mortgage payments to buy TV ads" for their business. (Susan Taylor Martin, "How Dare They Quit Paying Their Mortgage? Hey, That's Us!" *St. Petersburg Times*, June 9, 2010.)

† They were not alone: *The Wall Street Journal*, for example, profiled 30-year-old Derek Figg, who also decided to stop paying his mortgage: "Mr. Figg felt trapped in a home he bought two years ago in the Phoenix suburb of Tempe for $340,000. He still owes about $318,000 but figures the home's value has dropped to $230,000 or less. After agonizing over the pros and cons, he decided recently to stop making loan payments, even though he can afford them. Mr. Figg plans to rent an apartment nearby, saving about $700 a month." The *Journal* reported that such defaults were especially popular in Arizona, California, Florida, and Nevada. (James R. Hagerty and Nick Timiraos, "Debtor's Dilemma: Pay the Mortgage or Walk Away," *Wall Street Journal*, December 17, 2009.)

Shedding the Stigma

Predictably, *The New York Times* story generated a backlash. "It's sickening, really," wrote blogger Cassy Fiano. "There are people out there milking the system for all it's worth, taking no responsibility for their bad decisions, and then blaming the lenders when they end up in trouble. . . . Apparently, the right thing to do is to squat in a house you don't even fully own yet without paying what you legally owe."[3]

The vast majority of American homeowners agree with Fiano, but the Walk Away from Your Mortgage Movement was also gathering intellectual and journalistic momentum. The spread of strategic defaults illustrates the cascading effects of rewarding bad behavior, part of the "grab yours while you can" attitude that sometimes cloaks itself in the rhetoric of pseudo-Marxist egalitarianism, sometimes in the posture of hardheaded economic realism. Whether the argument is made from the left or the right, the case for stiffing lenders requires the rejection of the fusty middle-class morality that had led homeowners in the past to strive to pay off their mortgage even in the toughest times and the elimination of the lingering stigma against being a deadbeat.

In other contexts (most notably the stigmas against out-of-wedlock births or other forms of dependency) we've seen how quickly such stigmas can be eroded. The campaign to raze the remaining stigmas against defaulting on one's financial obligations is already under way in earnest.

Brett Arends, writing in *The Wall Street Journal,* urged millions of underwater homeowners "to stop living in a dream world and give serious thought to walking away from the debt." Arends noted that many people are "hung up on middle-class morality. But he offered absolution: Shame is naive in the current economic world. Arends concluded: "The economy is fundamentally amoral."[4]

Roger Lowenstein, in *The New York Times*, also rejected the notion that such defaults should be considered "antisocial and perhaps amoral." In a market society, he argued, "we are all economic pinballs, insensibly colliding for better or worse."[5]

But perhaps the strongest voice urging Americans to walk away is University of Arizona law professor Brent White, who frets that homeowners "should be walking away in droves. But they aren't."[6] And like Arends and Lowenstein, he blames the troublesome middle-class ethos of personal responsibility.

"It is time," declares White, "to take morals out of the picture and search for an equitable solution to the negative equity problem." Not only does Professor White want homeowners to get over their lingering sense of guilt, he goes further by suggesting they rev up their spending before they walk away from their mortgages, the better to enjoy their newfound freedom from responsibility. He suggests that defaulters can minimize the "marginal cost" of a trashed credit score by going on a spending binge before defaulting. "For example, one could purchase a new vehicle, secure a new home to rent, or even purchase a new house before beginning the process of defaulting on one's mortgage. Most individuals should be able to plan in advance for a few years of limited credit." Of course, this requires suppressing any lingering moral qualms, which is, of course, the whole point of the walk-away movement.

In his essay "Underwater and Not Walking Away," Professor White complains that society has discouraged homeowners from defaulting on their mortgages. "The clear message to American homeowners from nearly all fronts is that one has a moral responsibility to pay one's mortgage," writes White. "The message is conveyed not only by political, social, and economic institutions, but by the majority of Americans who believe that voluntarily default-ing on a mortgage is immoral. This stigma leads Americans to overemphasize the impact of a foreclosure on their credit." White argues that a bad credit score actually costs a few thousand dollars, far less than they would save by walking away from an underwater mortgage. But, complains White, middle-class Americans per-ceive it as a black mark to be avoided at almost all costs. "A bad credit score is—by design—meant to reflect not only one's poor creditworthiness," says White, "but also one's poor moral character." It is "nothing less than a reputational scarlet letter" that follows individuals wherever they go.

This is all quite unfair, he argues, because "norms governing homeowner behavior stand in sharp contrast to norms governing lenders, who seek to maximize profits or minimize losses irrespec-tive of concerns of morality or social responsibility." Meanwhile, "individual homeowners are encouraged to behave in accordance with social and moral norms requiring that individuals keep prom-ises and honor financial obligations."

One solution offered by White is to amend the Fair Credit Re-porting Act to bar lenders from reporting mortgage defaults and foreclosures to credit rating agencies. "Preventing lenders from reporting mortgage defaults to credit rating agencies would, as a practical matter, eliminate lenders' ability to hold borrowers' human worth as collateral." This would undoubtedly be successful in rais-ing the self-esteem of defaulters, but it would also render credit scores essentially useless as a guide to the creditworthiness and history of would-be borrowers. By making the lending process even less transparent than it now is, White's proposal would add even more uncertainty to the process, while setting the stage for precisely the sort of abuses that created the housing bubble in the first place. The whole point, after all, would be to make it easier for people to obtain loans even though they had reneged on previous commitments.

But White is looking for more than technical changes in credit reporting: He is also advocating a cultural sea change. "It is time to put to rest the assumption that a borrower who exercises the option to default is somehow immoral or irresponsible," he declares. "To the contrary, walking away may be the most financially responsible choice if it allows one to meet one's unsecured credit obligations or provide for the future economic stability of one's family. Individuals should not be artificially discouraged on the basis of 'morality' from making financially prudent decisions, particularly when the party on the other side is amorally operating according to market norms."

A Moral Obligation

But what exactly are those morals that White and the others so disdain? The critics specifically object to the belief that one should keep his promise, fulfill his obligations, and pay his debts if he is able to do so.

In fairness, some small businesses who tried to play by the rules were foreclosed upon by their banks, who also abdicated their responsibility to deal with them in good faith and thus undermined the sense of moral obligation on the part of other borrowers. This has potentially serious consequences because one of the most important factors in keeping the housing market afloat is precisely the imperative most Americans feel to live up to that moral obligation. The nation's culture of homeownership was based on a culture of such personal responsibility; the attitudes and values of middle-class America that made the single-family home the centerpiece of the American Dream are not separable from the middle-class sense of obligation that transcended issues of cash flow and made the market work for generations.

An influential study for the National Bureau of Economic Research documented the "surprising" importance of moral considerations in decisions about whether or not to default.[7] The study by Luigi Guiso, Paola Sapienza, and Luigi Zingales found that 80 percent of homeowners thought it was immoral to strategically default on a mortgage. Among those who had moral qualms, homeowners were 77 percent less likely to default than those who took the "amoral" position. The objections to walking away from mortgages was so powerful that the researchers found that only 17 percent of homeowners said they would walk away even if their equity fell to just 50 percent of the value of their house. "This moral barrier to default is an important and often ignored aspect of the default decision," they noted.* In other words, as White noted, "people are less likely to default if doing so will make them feel like immoral or irresponsible persons—and are especially unlikely to default if they believe others will think of them as immoral or irresponsible persons. Guilt and shame are powerful motivators."[8]

One study of foreclosures, for instance, interviewed a homeowner who worried about being seen as irresponsible: "And, um, so I'm just, I'm kind of interested in the public perception. You know I don't want to be a burden on the rest of society because I'm not paying my mortgage. Now there's this big giant bailout and I'm involved in that. You know, my mortgage was one of the mortgages not being paid."[9]

But as strong as the stigma against default was, the NBER study found that it could be eroded by two factors:

1. Public policies and bailouts that seem to subsidize irresponsible borrowing and that make homeowners who continue to

---

* The study found some variations in moral attitudes toward default: "Younger people (less than 35 years old) are less moral, but so are older ones (older than 65). More educated people exhibit less moral conviction as do African Americans. Wealthier people have higher moral standards, while people from the Northeast and the West less so."

pay their mortgages feel like suckers. "Moral norms, if widespread, may strongly mitigate the likelihood that American households will default on their mortgage, even if the value of housing continues to depreciate. The effectiveness of moral rules, in turn, may be affected by economic policies that may undermine a sense of fairness. . . . For example, a policy aimed at helping people in arrears with their mortgages could have devastating effects on the incentives to strategically default of people who can afford to pay their mortgage if it is perceived to bail out people unjustly and thus undermine the moral commitment to pay."

2. A breakdown in social norms, or what researchers referred to as "contagion effect that reduces the social stigma associated with default as defaults become more common." In other words, if people begin to see their neighbors walking away from their mortgages without suffering obvious negative consequences, they are more likely to do it themselves. The study found that "people who know someone who has strategically defaulted are 82% more likely to declare their intention to do so."[10]

Credit, Character, Culture

This is where economics meets morality and finance meets character and culture. White and others argue that the economy is fundamentally amoral and that it is time we all recognize the anachronism of middle-class concepts of responsibility and moral reciprocity. Ultimately the issue comes down to the question: Why do we pay our debts? Because it is convenient for us, or because it is in our economic interest to do so, or because it is the right thing to do?

Paying what one owes, like keeping one's word even if it is inconvenient, is a sign of personal responsibility and a marker of good character. If it were not, we would make no social or moral distinction between the spendthrift deadbeat and the responsible and trustworthy. In that sense economic arrangements reflect social norms and vice versa: Debt is a moral as well as a financial exchange. Remove the connection between character and financial trustworthiness and the system is changed in fundamental ways; so is the cultural fabric and the social contract on which the American economy has been built.

What happens, though, if the moral stigma is removed? What happens if financial responsibility is decoupled from notions of "good character"? Such a transformation means that a promise to pay a debt becomes, instead, a dare: Lend me money and I will repay if it is convenient to me.

The advocates of walking away from your mortgage would respond that this does not account for the provision of collateral: The homeowner promises to pay the mortgage *or surrender the property to the bank*. But the point of strategic default is to choose to not pay back the amount borrowed (plus interest). The moral and financial reluctance to renege on such loans is not much different from the moral objection to refusing to pay other debts, which might also be inconvenient. During a recession, for instance, heavy credit card debt can also be an annoying drain on cash flow even for borrowers with sufficient income to pay such debt. Since those credit card balances are largely unsecured, such debt is by definition always "underwater." The same applies to many auto loans, which may exceed the book value of the car, truck, or van they helped to purchase. Why wouldn't the same amoral logic apply to strategic defaults on all of these promissory notes, especially since we are supposed to be getting past this whole idea of "promises"?

Unfortunately, moral arguments alone will not determine the direction that American culture and finance takes in the next few decades. Applying the "sucker principle" to the mortgage issue, homeowners will react to how government and their neighbors behave. If playing by the rules and paying one's mortgage out of a sense of moral obligation comes to seem like a sucker's game, if government subsidizes deadbeats and defaulting becomes both common and socially acceptable (or at least not objectionable), the culture of responsibility will have reached a tipping point.

An Interactive Reader's Exercise

✳ ✳ ✳

Try your hand at rewriting (and updating) this classic story of the Ant and the Grasshopper to fit modern circumstances.

In the original story, the Grasshopper spends his summer pursuing his bliss, while the Ant works hard to prepare for the future.

One day as the Ant walks by, laboriously hauling a kernel of corn, the Grasshopper jibes: "Where are you off to with that heavy thing?"

The Ant replies that he is taking it to his Anthill.

The Grasshopper scoffs and invites the Ant to party with him, instead of working so hard.

The Ant patiently explains that he is working hard to prepare for winter and suggests that the Grasshopper do the same.

"Why bother about winter?" answers the Grasshopper. "We have plenty of food right now."

But, of course, summer doesn't last; the temperatures fall, and snow covers the fields, burying whatever food may have been left there.

The Grasshopper soon finds himself both cold and hungry.

He heads to the Ant's hill and finds him handing out the corn that he has collected all summer.

According to the traditional story, the Grasshopper then realizes: "It is best to prepare for the days of necessity."

✳   ✳   ✳

What would he say now?

Feel free to work in modern agriculture subsidies (which pay farmers for not growing and hand out cash for "disasters"), unemployment compensation, disability payments, and food stamps, as well as other transfer payments or bailouts the Grasshopper may have received.

Also feel free to add any other programs that might "spread the wealth," from the Ant "haves" to the Grasshopper "have nots."

_____

_____

_____

_____

_____

_____

_____

_____

_____

_____

_____

_____

Chapter 13

NO, THEY DIDN'T LEARN ANYTHING

By and large the mortgage bailout effort has failed, perhaps reflecting the inherent difficulties in trying to turn the unaffordable into the affordable simply by government fiat or intervention. Nearly 60 percent of the delinquent mortgages that were modified by banks were in default again within the first year.[1] As it turns out, not surprisingly, reckless deals can seldom be transformed into viable ones, even by acts of Congress. It was not, however, for lack of trying and tens of billions of dollars of taxpayer money.

In February 2009, President Obama declared that his $75 billion Home Affordable Modification Program (HAMP) would "enable as many as three to four million homeowners to modify the terms of their mortgages to avoid foreclosure."[2] The idea was to provide an incentive for lenders to modify troubled mortgages. Within the program's first year, 40 percent of the 1.5 million people who tried HAMP were booted from the program altogether, and the whole process became known colloquially as "extend and pretend." Rather than saving homes from foreclosure, the program only delayed the inevitable. As two financial writers for *The Huffington Post* explained, by "extending the process by which homes enter foreclosure" banks were allowed to carry the loans on their books at full value, which "allows unhealthy banks to appear healthy, staving off costly bank failures." Or, in other words, pretend to be solvent.

But there comes a day when all fairy tales and attempts at financial self-deception come to an end. Or at least you'd think so.

No Down Payment, No Income

Even as the economy was trying to crawl back from the subprime lending meltdown, the taxpayer-funded Wisconsin Housing and Economic Development Authority ran radio ads touting no-money-down mortgages:

> WHEDA . . . We do . . . So you can buy your first house with no money down! Coming up with a down payment prevents a lot of renters from becoming homeowners. . . ."

What if you also have no income? Not to worry. There was a bailout for that, too. WHEDA promised that the taxpayers would even pay your mortgage for six months if you lose your job. At first, the new loan program known as Affordable Advantage was offered in just three states: Massachusetts, Minnesota, and Wisconsin. Because the states unloaded the mortgages to Fannie Mae, *The New York Times* noted, "taxpayers are on the hook if the loans go bad."[3]

That includes loans in which homeowners paid as little as 67 cents down. One of the early borrowers under the Wisconsin program was a couple named Matthew and Hannah Middlebrooke, who bought a $115,000 three-bedroom ranch house with a down payment of just $1,000. But because the couple also got a grant to cover closing costs and insurance, they ended up at the closing writing out a check for just 67 cents.

Commenting on the return of the government-sponsored virtually-no-down-payment loans, CNBC's Diana Olick noted that the program "seems contradictory in its fundamental premise. The buyers in the Affordable Advantage program have no skin in the game from the start, and no guarantee that the home won't lose value over the next year."[4] One of the directors of the Government Accountability Office reminded *The New York Times* that "loans that have zero down payment perform worse than loans with down payments. . . . And loans with down payment assistance"—like those being marketed by the housing agencies–"perform worse than those that do not."[5]

Isn't this how we got into this mess in the first place?

TARPing the (Upper) Middle Class

In March 2010, the Treasury Department announced yet another attempt to beef up its bailout program by throwing even more cash at it. The Treasury hoped that with a taxpayer subsidy, some lenders might provide mortgage relief for homeowners who were underwater on their mortgages. One provision required mortgage providers to write off a portion of mortgage loans to get them down to "a manageable level." As *The New York Times* reported, "To lubricate its efforts, the government plans to spread taxpayers' money around liberally."[6]

Who was eligible for this latest round of taxpayer generosity? The Treasury Department explained that you could tap the HAMP if you:

> live in an owner occupied principal residence, *have a mortgage balance of less than $729,750*, owe monthly mortgage payments that are not affordable (greater than 31 percent of their income) and demonstrate a financial hardship. The new flexibilities for the modification initiative announced today continue to target this group of homeowners.[7] (Emphasis added.)

Pause here, and then reread that.

Economist Keith Hennessey was flabbergasted. Even by the ever-eroding standards of the bailout tsunami, this was stunning. Under the government's plan, calculated Hennessey, homeowners with annual incomes of up to $186,000 a year would be eligible for the assistance. The price tag: $50 billion.

Asked Hennessey: "Does it really make sense for the Administration to use taxpayer funds to subsidize someone making less than $186,000 per year to stay in a home with a $700,000 mortgage balance?!"[8]

"This isn't even a middle-class entitlement," commented finance writer Lawrence Kudlow, "it's an upper-middle-class entitlement."[9]

Hennessey challenged the premise behind bailing out "underwater" homeowners. Many of those homeowners had, of course, suffered traumatic losses in the value of their homes, but if they had fixed-rate mortgages, their actual out-of-pocket costs wouldn't be affected. The homeowner could stay in the house and wait for the price to edge back up, just as an investor might hold on to an undervalued stock.

Why, then, Hennessey asked, should the taxpayers subsidize a homeowner who has lost money on a real-estate investment any more than taxpayers should subsidize someone who lost money on a bad stock bet? "Why do policymakers (on both sides of the aisle) think we should make taxpayers (some of whom struggle to make their own mortgage payments, and others of whom rent housing) subsidize someone who lost money on an investment?"

He suggests this scenario: "Two twin brothers each make $180,000 a year. One rents, and the other has a $700,000 mortgage on a home that declined from $800,000 in value to $600,000 in value. Both brothers lose their jobs. Why should the renter pay higher taxes to subsidize his brother's mortgage payments?"

Hennessey offered this kicker: Imagine a third brother (who also rents) and who loses $200,000 in the stock market, "and explain how your policy applies to him."[10]

Part Five

MIDDLE-CLASS SUCKERS

Chapter 14

THE BANK OF MOM AND DAD

Tucked inside the massive health-care reform bill of 2010 was a symbolic cultural declaration: The new law allows children to stay on their parents' health insurance plan up to the age of 26. In a sense, the law was simply catching up with the trend toward delayed adulthood as more twenty-somethings fail to launch.

But the bill also was a milestone: It codified in federal law the dramatic shift in the age at which young people should be considered independent by legally extending the right to continue to mooch off Mom and Dad for an additional half-decade. As more and more young people take a leisurely journey to adulthood, the ages of 18 and 21 increasingly lack relevance for the actual path to independence. With a stroke of the pen, 26 has become the new 18.

In an earlier book, I wrote: "Previous generations crossed the frozen Bering Straits, rounded the Cape of Good Hope, discovered the New World, traveled the Oregon Trail, climbed Mount Everest." The Greatest Generation included teenage boys who went off to liberate Europe, island-hop through the Pacific, and defeat the Japanese Empire.[1]

"So far, though, the great pioneering move of Generation Me is to move back home to live with Mom." This was perhaps somewhat unfair, but the failure to launch among young adults has become so widespread that it has inspired its own euphemisms: "emerging adults," thresholders, twixters, and kidults. None of them should be taken as compliments.

Somehow previous generations were able to grow up more quickly under far worse conditions. So did their parents, who not only didn't have the Internet and cable television, but may have felt themselves lucky to have their own bedroom and indoor plumbing. But they grew up, and if they did live with their parents, they were probably helping to support the seniors, not the other way around.

A great deal of impressive scholarship has been arrayed to explain why the younger generation is delaying adulthood into their late twenties and even into their thirties. Traditionally, young people couldn't wait to get out of the house, get their own place, and experience the freedom and pride of self-sufficiency and self-reliance. But now so many are failing or refusing to leave home that sociologists and demographers have had to redefine adulthood itself. In 2004 a team of social scientists concluded that "it takes much longer to make the transition to adulthood today than decades ago, and arguably longer than it has in any time in American history."[2]

Explanations abound: Changes in the economy, the increasing importance and length of higher education, and delays in marriage and childbearing certainly play major roles in the postponement of adulthood. Even though most Americans think the age of 21 remains a key milestone, the MacArthur Foundation's Network on Transitions to Adulthood notes that in reality, by age 21, "few young people today would actually be considered 'adult' based on the traditional markers—leaving home, finishing school, starting a job, getting married, and having children. More youth are extending education, living at home longer, and moving haltingly, or stopping altogether, along the stepping stones of adulthood."[3] In the 1960s, 37 to 40 percent of young adults finished school, left home, got jobs, married, and had children. Today the routes are more idiosyncratic. According to the Network on Transitions study, the number of young adults who follow that path had dropped to 25 to 29 percent in the 1990s.*[4]

The "more ambiguous and extended path" they are taking means that many young adults who are technically past the age of majority have no idea what to do with themselves. The study found that "fewer young people at age 22, much less someone in their teens, know what they are going to do in the next 10 years than they did even a few decades ago."

Sooner or later, of course, they will have to grow up, stop mooching off their parents, and actually move out of the house. But apparently not yet.

The number of so-called boomerangs—adult children between the ages of 18 and 24 who move back home—is up by 50 percent since 1970. Census figures suggest that 56 percent of men and 43 percent of women between the ages of 18 and 24 continue to live with a parent. Even more continue to rely on the bank of Mom and Dad, well past the age when grown-ups were once expected to pay their own way.

Send Money

"Helicopter parents" have made themselves unavoidable presences throughout academe and even (cringingly) in the workplace. So

---

* The median age for a first marriage has risen from 23 in 1980 to 27 for men and 26 for women; almost all racial and income groups report a delay in childbearing.

called because of their tendency to hover and overprotect their children, the helicopter parent has become an iconic figure of postmodern culture, representing a new sort of parent who never . . . lets . . . go. A plague on college administrators, these parents are so omnipresent at orientation sessions that some schools have had to develop tactics for shooing them off campus so that their children can get on with the business of higher education.

But just as helicopter parents are reluctant to let go simply because a child goes off to college, many parents seem reluctant to encourage or even allow their children to become financially independent. Understandably, many young adults are fine with this. Increasingly parents do not merely follow their children on Facebook, but also routinely pay their bills well into their thirties.

According to the MacArthur study, adults between 18 and 34 receive an average of $38,000 in cash from their parents, "and . . . this support has increased substantially in the last decades."[5]

The cash, reported *The New York Times*, "helps to pay for housing, bills and travel expenses, and the support has been increasing for the past two decades as education is extended, marriage is delayed and young people take the scenic route from adolescence to adulthood."[6]

Researchers Robert Schoeni and Karen Ross put this in perspective: Middle-class parents can spend $190,980 raising a child through age 17, according to 2005 government statistics, but they will probably spend another $42,280 (in 2005 dollars) over the next seventeen years. Obviously that includes the cost of higher education, but it is not limited to tuition. Their research found that on average, middle-class parents were paying $2,323 a year to subsidize offspring 25 and 26 years old.[7]

The contributions are not limited to cash. Nearly half of young adults (18 to 34) who live away from home report receiving noncash assistance from their parents in the form of time, such as "driving them home to the city after a visit, doing laundry, taking care of grandchildren."

According to Schoeni and Ross, this parental time assistance amounts to an average of 367 hours, the equivalent of nine weeks of full-time mommy and daddy work.

"The bottom line," noted the *Times*, "is that the assumption that financial obligations to children ended after graduation from high school or college is going the way of the pay phone."[8]

Extending Dependency

Not all of this is bad, of course. The delay of childbearing and more and better education are often good choices that ought to be encouraged, but there are troubling implications as well. The delay of adulthood suggests a declining premium on independence among the young, for with the parental subsidies come strings. Avoiding those strings has long been the goal of young people leaving the nest. For many, however, the lengthening path to adulthood means the extension of parental involvement, and ultimately control. Most young people of previous generations were reluctant to make the tradeoff, but an increasing number of the younger population appear quite comfortable with it.

One result is that adults—even those in the middle and upper middle classes—spend less time being economically independent and a larger portion of their lives dependent on others.

This shift has significant demographic and political implications: If 30 is the new 20, the time a worker will be economically self-sufficient can be cut by nearly a fourth unless they stay employed a decade longer. As the younger generation takes the "scenic route" to adulthood, the burden of supporting the economy will be pushed onto an even smaller slice of productive taxpayers. (This was the generation that boomers were counting on to support them in their retirement. Disappointment seems inevitable, although they may get their revenge when young adults make the transition from moocher to mooched upon.) Statistics on income and wealth will also be skewed as the number of people (even those from affluent backgrounds and with expensive educations) who will be counted as "low income" is inflated.

Politically, the delay in adulthood means the shift of millions of individuals, who would otherwise have experienced the joys of tax withholding, into a prolonged period of dependency—not just on Mom and Dad, but also on programs that enable them to pursue what Fred Siegel called "dependent individualism." (See "Hungry Hipsters" in Chapter 6.) Such dependency establishes not only a habit but also a constituency for programs of support by expanding and extending the pool of takers.

Chapter 15

MIDDLE-CLASS SUCKERS

Three stories:

- In Wisconsin, if a single mother with two children who makes $15,000 a year marries the father of her children, who makes $30,000 a year, a legislator calculates, "she will lose government benefits totaling $37,000 per year."[1]

- Two classmates both take out $40,000 in student loans. Student A takes time off to find himself and then takes a minimum-wage job at a nonprofit group devoted to saving the iguanas. Student B gets a job in engineering and makes $70,000 a year. Student A pays $47 a month on his student loan; Student B pays $672. Student A is also eligible for the Earned Income Tax Credit program and food stamps and gets free medical care. After ten years working for Save the Iguanas, Student A also will have his loan completely forgiven under the "public service loan forgiveness" provision of his loan. Student B will have to pay off the full balance of his loan, plus interest.[2]

- Under the new health care bill, a middle-class couple in their forties who get a raise from $93,000 to $94,000 in 2014 could see their net income fall drastically as they lose more than $8,800 in federal subsidies for their health insurance. By getting the small raise, more than a quarter of their net income will go to pay premiums.[3] They will, of course, also be paying federal and state taxes to subsidize other people's coverage.

The reverse is also true in each case: If the Wisconsin woman refuses to marry the father of her children, she can keep her $37,000 share of government aid. The student who gets a well-paying job can quit and let taxpayers subsidize his student loan; a middle-class couple who decides to cut their income will be able to increase their health subsidy by thousands of dollars.

For both the poor and the middle class, the array of means-tested programs often means that more is less because they have benefits that phase out as income rises. Some of those benefits fall off a cliff—all the way to zero—if individuals or families make even a dollar more. Even without increases in marginal tax rates, the effect can be huge penalties for effort and success.

At some point for both groups, the American Dream no longer makes sense because of the perverse incentives: The more you earn, the less you can cadge from the taxpayers, which in many ways mirrors the effects of progressive taxation under which the more you earn, the less you get to keep. In some cases there is an actual tipping point where a higher income can leave both the poor and middle class worse off financially.

Welcome to the Muddle Class

In October 2009, *Forbes* magazine devoted its cover story to an eye-opening examination of the middle-class squeeze: "When Work Doesn't Pay for the Middle Class." The article featured a 50-year-old single mother who was seriously considering taking a job that paid her half the $120,000 salary she had earned at her last job as a publicity manager. The choice to take a 50 percent pay cut reflected the tight job market, but also "makes sense when you consider how this country punishes work effort."[4]

Explained *Forbes*: "While the first $60,000 of her income would be lightly taxed, the next $60,000 would be hit with what is in effect a 79% tax rate. Given a choice between a part-time or easy job paying $60,000 and a demanding, stress-ridden job paying $120,000," the woman would be better off taking the former. Why? The authors ran the numbers:

"At $120,000 she would pay $16,500 a year more in federal and state taxes, wouldn't qualify for the five-year $12,000-a-year cut in her mortgage payments she's applying for and would be eligible for $19,000 a year less in need-based college financial aid."

There are more than two dozen federal tax breaks that decline and eventually disappear when income goes up. When the woman's income increased from $60,000 to $90,000, for example, she would lose some or all of the per-child credit, the college student credit, the Making Work Pay credit, eligibility for a homebuyer credit, along with deductions for her IRA and for student loan interest. Especially for the middle class, noted *Forbes*, the tax code has become "a blatant shell game. Congress gives with one hand and takes with the other."[5]

The Parent
(and Student) Tax

The big hammer, however, is the cost of college, an especially tricky and onerous problem for the middle class. To qualify for need-based financial aid, parents have to be careful not to make too much and not to have too much saved. Generally a family with the misfortune to make more than $65,000 a year is expected to pay out 47 percent of their after-tax income and a portion of their savings to the cause of higher education. "A few rich universities cut the poor and even the middle class more slack," noted *Forbes*. "A family earning $65,000 whose kid gets into Princeton will have to kick in maybe $2,000, and the contribution rate rises gently from there. Still, by $150,000 in income or so, parents are back to that 47% aid tax."

Which brings us back to the 50-year-old single mom, who found that reaching her full income potential was very likely a sucker's game.

The tax on success will not stop when her daughter graduates from college. Under the "income-based repayment plan" for federal student loans, the amount her daughter pays back—or whether she pays all of it back at all—could depend on how successful she is at avoiding well-paying jobs.

Think of the system as a crash course on "How to Borrow Money Without Paying It Back." First, you borrow the money. Then, if you work at jobs that pay low enough, you can make only token payments for ten years. If you have been fortunate enough to avoid the private sector, working instead for a nonprofit or for government, the balance of the loan is canceled. Actually, the debt is not wiped away; it is simply paid for by taxpayers. The loan becomes a gift. Given the generous salaries and lavish benefits of government jobs, it's not clear how this additional benefit is justified, but it is certainly valuable. Under the income-based plan, a student's monthly payments would be capped depending on income: A single person making $15,000 would pay nothing on the loan, while a single classmate who made $65,000 a year would pay up to $609 a month on the same loan. Conversely, a student who decides to quit her job to wait tables or sweep streets for the local government could save herself thousands of dollars a year.[6]

The Mother of All
Tax Credits

The incentives for the poor can be even more upside down: A poor individual who marries or takes a better job or gets a raise is at risk of losing food stamps, health care coverage, child care subsidies, and the Earned Income Tax Credit. As the left-leaning National Center for Children in Poverty (NCCP) notes, "The result is that parents can work and earn more without their families moving closer to financial security."[7]

The NCCP uses the example of a single mother named Becky who makes $16,000 a year. If she somehow increases her income to $36,000, she will lose her government subsidy for child care. If she continues to improve her lot in life, her children may lose health coverage and she will lose the cash she gets from the Earned Income Credit.

We find a similar effect in the case of the Wisconsin woman cited at the beginning of this chapter. How does a single mother lose $37,000 in benefits simply by getting married? A Wisconsin legislator, Glenn Grothman, crunched the numbers on the state's programs for low-income families. Start with the Earned Income

Credit: Because the mom makes less than $34,458 a year, she is eligible for a check from the government worth about $4,820. If she gets married, he noted, she loses the entire check.

Similarly, when it comes to the state's low-income health care program, the mom is only eligible as long as her income is less than 185 percent of the federal poverty level; unless she gets married, she qualifies for the program, which has a benefit worth about $3,300 a year. She is also eligible for roughly $9,200 a year in day care benefits as long as her income stays below $33,876. If she marries, the income limit rises to $40,788, but since she and the father make more than that, they would lose the benefit. The mom would also lose low-income housing assistance, food stamps, and energy assistance, and her children would no longer be eligible for Milwaukee's private school choice program. This doesn't include other benefits such as subsidized school lunches. With those incentives, who would get married?

"No wonder 41 percent of American births last year were to single women," wrote Grothman.[8]

Ironically, advocates for the poor cite an effect similar to high marginal tax rates to explain the disincentives to marriage and work in the current system. "For example," notes the NCCP, "if three benefits each phase out at a rate of $.30 for each $1 of earnings, the cumulative effect could be that an additional dollar of earnings results in a loss of $.90 in benefits, leaving only a $.10 gain. This is the equivalent of a 90 percent 'marginal tax rate.'"[9] Of course, it is not a tax at all, but the point is provocative: Faced with losing 90 cents of every dollar earned, why would anyone want to get a promotion, work more hours, or get married?

This was not the original idea. The Earned Income Tax Credit was supposed to make work pay and help the working poor rise into the middle class, which perhaps explains its strong bipartisan support. Over time the "credit" has become the country's second-largest public assistance program behind only Medicaid; and according to government auditors the credit is among the most fraud-ridden program in history.[10]

It is, first of all, not a credit at all: The EITC can be a straight-out transfer payment. Low-income individuals who otherwise pay no income taxes file tax returns so they can get the government check of up to $5,617. (In 2007 the average benefit for a family with children was $2,488.)[11] There is no time limit for participation in the program; recipients can access taxpayer cash year in and year out, world without end. One study found that half of all families with children tap in to the tax credit at one time or another.[12] More than 25 million EITC returns are filed every year, costing taxpayers who pay in to the government more than $40 billion in transfer payments.

The scope of the cheating is massive: In 2005, the Government Accountability Office found that "the IRS estimated between 5.5 and 7.3 million fraudulent payments a year at a cost to taxpayers of somewhere between $11 billion and $14.6 billion."[13]

But the greatest effect of the tax "credit" and other phased-out benefits is on the incentives.

"Don't think the American public is stupid," *Forbes* magazine quoted a tax practitioner saying of the credits. "People call me and say, 'What's the most I can earn before I lose the earned income tax credit?' [They] may not understand marginal rates, but they're shocked when they lose the college or child credits. You hear all the time, 'The harder I work, the more they take away from me.'"[14]

The Health Care Cliff

The new health care reform bill will also dramatically change the financial landscape for the middle class. Long before Obamacare was a gleam in Congress's eye, the habit of individuals paying for their own medical care had virtually disappeared from the American economy. Even otherwise responsible adults came to regard the notion of actually paying out of pocket for routine health maintenance as anathema. The result has been the separation of the medical consumer from the actual cost of his or her treatment, a significant contributor to the rise in health care costs. Car insurance, for instance, does not cover changing the windshield wiper blade, or the oil; it is reserved for more catastrophic injuries or damages. The average car owner assumes that he will bear the cost of buying windshield wiper fluid or replacing a burnt-out taillight. Not so with health insurance.

The "reform" bill passed in 2010 created a new system in which taxpayers get to subsidize hundreds of billions of dollars of other people's health care—other people who are by definition neither elderly nor poor, since they were already covered by taxpayer-funded health programs like Medicare and Medicaid. Apart from its effect on the nation's health care system (which is beyond the scope of this book), the legislation extends government subsidies and incentives deep into the middle class, with results that may only be realized in the coming years.

Because the new health care law includes powerful incentives for employers to drop their health coverage, many employees may find themselves pushed into the new insurance exchanges. And for many of them, the initial shift may seem like a good deal. Starting in 2014, a 46-year-old head of a family of four who makes $40,000 a year, for example, will get a government (read taxpayer) subsidy of $16,032 a year to buy a government-approved policy. But, like other credits, the health insurance subsidy phases out as income rises, then drops off a cliff.

This is how it will work for the family of four headed by a 46-year-old policy holder, according to the Kaiser Family Foundation's subsidy calculator:[15]

Family One

Annual income (in 2014 dollars): $30,000

Unsubsidized health insurance premium: $0 (covered under Medicaid)

Actual out-of-pocket premium: $0 (Medicaid)

Government tax credit: Medicaid

Family Two

Annual income (in 2014 dollars): $44,000

Unsubsidized health insurance premium: $17,766

Actual out-of-pocket premium: $2,526

Government tax credit: $15,240

Family Three

Annual income (in 2014 dollars): $64,000

Unsubsidized health insurance premium: $17,766

Actual out-of-pocket premium: $5,583

Government tax credit: $12,183

Family Four

Annual income (in 2014 dollars): $84,000

Unsubsidized health insurance premium: $17,766

Actual out-of-pocket premium: $7,980

Government tax credit: $9,786

Now we approach the cliff.

Family Five has an annual 2014 income of $93,000—397 percent of the poverty line—and this is the way it looks:

Unsubsidized health insurance premium: $17,766

Actual out-of-pocket premium: $8,835

Government tax credit: $8,931

If that family increases its annual income by just $1,000—to 401 percent of poverty—this is how the numbers change:

Annual income (in 2014 dollars): $94,000
Unsubsidized health insurance premium: $17,766
Actual out-of-pocket premium: $17,766
Government tax credit: $0

In other words, that additional $1,000 in income costs the family more than $8,900 in after-tax income . . . *a marginal tax of more than 890 percent.* Instead of paying $8,800 or so for their health insurance premium, the tab becomes $17,766. (Actually, the dividing line is hit precisely at $93,700, which is 400 percent of poverty. In other words, a $100 raise is enough to trigger the loss of the $89,800 subsidy . . . a marginal rate of 8,900 percent.*

As the American Enterprise Institute's Scott Gottlieb points out, the new system will mean that after taxes, a family making $100,000 a year will be "spending almost a quarter of their net income for health insurance."[16] They will not be able to refuse to buy the policy, nor will substantially cheaper policies be available. (Some may choose to go without insurance at all, opting to pay Obamacare's fine instead.) Meanwhile, many of their neighbors will be paying

---

* The Kaiser Family Foundation explains its health reform subsidy calculator: "Based on the Patient Protection and Affordable Care Act (including subsequent amendments in the Health Care and Education Reconciliation Act of 2010), as signed by the President. . . .

"The premiums are illustrative examples in 2014 dollars derived from estimates of average premiums for 2016 from the Congressional Budget Office. For a 40 year old single adult, the premium for a silver plan is assumed to be $4,500 for a plan with a 70% actuarial value. To the extent that actual expected enrollment in 2014 differs from what CBO assumed for 2016—e.g., it has a different composition of people by health status or age—then premiums could vary from this amount.

"Premium subsidies are based on a silver plan (with an actuarial value of 70%), so all premiums shown are for silver coverage. People may be able to pay a lower premium for less comprehensive coverage (i.e., a bronze plan, with an actuarial value of 60%). The tables showing results by age and income also reflect premiums for silver coverage, though the minimum insurance that people would be required to obtain would be bronze coverage."

little or nothing, because the "richer" families will be paying for them as well.

How will this change the middle class, besides imposing vast new costs on them? It hardly seems far-fetched to suggest that many families will choose to forgo, even actively avoid, extra income, the better to get in on the growing largesse of the taxpayers. In order to not give up government aid, more Americans may avoid marriage, second jobs, even promotions and overtime, thus dampening the creation and expansion of small business. For many members of the middle class, the sucker's principle comes into play: Why make more money when the government is handing out even more?

But perhaps the most important effect will be to extend dependence on government aid deep into the middle class (which was perhaps the point all along). As the middle class begins to realize that its pursuit of happiness in the traditional American sense merely turns them into piggy banks, Moocher Nation will have reached yet another tipping point.

Chapter 16

WHY GET A JOB?

Politicians are continuously surprised to learn that many people prefer to get something for free rather than having to work for it. Faced with persistent unemployment, their first reaction has been to extend unemployment benefits, despite warnings from economists that the subsidies may actually prolong joblessness. In July 2010, Congress ventured into previously uncharted waters by extending unemployment insurance for the fourth time, to up to ninety-nine weeks in some high-unemployment states, including Michigan, where employers had already noticed something peculiar: Despite double-digit unemployment, jobless men were turning down perfectly good jobs so that they could continue collecting unemployment checks.

Reported *The Detroit News*: "In a state with the nation's highest jobless rate, landscaping companies are finding some job applicants are rejecting work offers so they can continue collecting unemployment benefits." The paper suggested that the number of seasonal workers avoiding jobs "raises questions about whether extended unemployment benefits give the jobless an incentive to avoid work."[1]

One executive of a landscaping company in Warren, Michigan, said he had had about a dozen job offers refused. "One applicant, who had eight weeks to go until his state unemployment benefits ran out, asked for a deferred start date."

Surprising? Do the math: In Michigan the average unemployment check was about $255 a week. If an unemployed worker went to work at a landscaping company, he would likely make $225 more than that. But after taxes, the gap between couch and work shrinks to just $95 a week.

So is the additional $95 worth going to work 40 hours a week? In the heat? And the dirt? And the gasoline fumes? For many workers the answer, unsurprisingly, was no. As the *Detroit News* reported, one former landscaper who had been on unemployment for a year said he didn't plan on returning to work until the benefits ran out. "It's crazy," he said. "They keep doing all of these extensions."

Some workers aren't content to merely milk the system. The *News* reported that some job applicants asked to be paid in cash "so they can collect unemployment illegally." One contractor complained that the system was encouraging "more and more people and companies to play the system and get paid or collect cash money so they don't have to pay taxes."[2]

Economists confirm what common sense suggests: When you can pocket 50 to 60 percent or more of your salary for doing absolutely nothing, many workers will prefer sitting on the couch to returning to work. Moreover, extending the benefits tends to extend the time on the couch, while the expiration of the payments (not surprisingly) turns out to be a motivating factor in getting workers back to work.

Even members of the Obama administration have acknowledged as much. In 1995 economic adviser Lawrence Summers co-authored a paper with James Poterba of the Massachusetts Institute of Technology (MIT) that concluded: "Unemployment insurance lengthens unemployment spells."[3]

Even though he would later serve in an administration that repeatedly sought to extend unemployment benefits, Summers provided a clear illustration of the ways government provided an incentive not to work. Summers argued that every unemployed worker has what he called a "reservation wage," by which he meant the minimum wage that workers will have to get before accepting a job. Noted Summers: "Unemployment insurance and other social assistance programs increase that reservation wage, causing an unemployed person to remain unemployed longer."

Summers broke it down this way: Imagine an unemployed person who had made $15 an hour before losing his or her job. Unemployment insurance, Summers noted, would replace about 55 percent of the lost income, or about $8.25 an hour. Assuming the worker is in the 15 percent tax bracket and pays a 3 percent state tax, "he or she pays $1.49 in taxes per hour not worked and nets $6.76 per hour after taxes as compensation for not working."*

What would they net if they actually took a job at their old wage? Summers asked. Again, the workers would pay a combined income tax rate of 18 percent, plus an additional 7.65 percent for payroll taxes. That would leave the newly reemployed worker with a net of $11.15 an hour. The difference then between work and unemployment was $4.39 an hour. The unemployed, wrote Summers, could well decide that "an hour of leisure is worth more than the extra $4.39 the job would pay." That would also mean that his

---

* Summers was using pre–Bush tax cut numbers, but some state income taxes can actually be higher than the one he assumed.

or her "reservation wage" would be above $15 per hour. "Unemployment, therefore," Summer concluded, "may not be as costly for the jobless person as previously imagined."[4]*

Summer's analysis was confirmed in 2002 when Assistant Secretary of the Treasury for Economic Policy Alan Krueger and Bruce Meyer of the University of Chicago found that "unemployment insurance and worker's compensation insurance . . . tend to increase the length of time employees spend out of work."[5] Professor Meyer has written that "the probability of leaving unemployment rises dramatically just prior to when benefits lapse."[6] In other words, the jobless behave rationally. They will take the benefit as long as they can and only start seriously looking to go back to work when it runs out.[†]

Harvard economist Robert Barro notes that "generous unemployment-insurance programs have been found to raise unemployment in many Western European countries in which unemployment rates have been far higher than the current U.S. rate." Despite this, the Obama administration continued to extend eligibility to nearly two years from the standard twenty-six weeks. As a result, "We have shifted toward a welfare program

---

* Wrote Summers: "But as Harvard economist Martin Feldstein pointed out in the 1970s, the costs of unemployment to taxpayers are very great indeed. Take the example above of the individual who could work for $15.00 an hour or collect unemployment insurance of $8.25 per hour. The cost of unemployment to this unemployed person was only $4.39 per hour, the difference between the net income from working and the net income from not working. And as compensation for this cost, the unemployed person gained leisure, whose value could well be above $4.39 per hour. But other taxpayers as a group paid $8.25 in unemployment benefits for every hour the person was unemployed, and got back in taxes only $1.49 on this benefit. Moreover, they gave up $3.85 in lost tax and Social Security revenue that this person would have paid per hour employed at a $15.00 wage. Net loss to other taxpayers: $10.61 ($8.25 − $1.49 + $3.85) per hour. Multiply this by millions of people collecting unemployment, each missing hundreds of hours of work, and you get a cost to taxpayers in the billions."

† Meyer and Lawrence Katz of Harvard estimated that "a one-week increase in potential benefit duration increases the average duration of the unemployment spells . . . by 0.16 to 0.20 weeks." (Lawrence H. Summers, "Unemployment," *The Concise Encyclopedia of Economics*, www.econlib.org/library/Enc/Unemployment.html.)

that resembles those in many Western European countries." Noting that the jobless remain on the dole far longer during the current recession, Barro believes that the unprecedented extension of the benefits has contributed to the slowness of the recovery. Barro argues that without the generous stay-at-home benefit, the unemployment rate would have been 6.8 rather than 9.6 percent in the fall of 2010.[7]

Chapter 17

MOOCHING OFF THE KIDS

TRENTON—Over the last eighteen months, a New Jersey woman ran up six-figure debts in the names of her five children, ages 3 to 17.

According to court records, Carmela Jennings purchased a $1.2 million home in Camden, New Jersey, taking out mortgages in the names of her two youngest children, Lindsay and Tina, aged 3 and 5. Records show that Jennings also purchased a Mercedes CLS class car in the name of her son Jed. Jed is unlikely to drive the $85,000 car, since he is 10 years old.

Jennings also applied for and was issued credit cards in the name of each of the children, using them to pay for landscaping on her house, a $75,000 gazebo in her backyard, and

$65,000 in cosmetic surgery, including tummy tucks and breast implants . . . all charged to her children.

Authorities said that Jennings had told the other children and family members that she was making regular payments into a college fund for the children, but in fact, Jennings drained the inheritances the children had received from their grandparents and used it to pay for the installation of a new indoor swimming pool, outdoor hot tub, a basement home theater system, and paving a 1500-ft. driveway. Jennings also purchased a $35,000 model high-speed train set, also charged to her kids.

Jennings, a social worker, apparently also had a generous side. Records indicate that she purchased recreational vehicles for her three brothers, Eugene, Guido, and Sonny, and apparently fully funded the retirement accounts of four of her cousins. Because they all borrowed against their IRAs, none of the cousins reports any remaining balance. All of the costs were charged to Jennings's children.

State authorities say that each child now apparently owes between $275,000 and $700,000 in debts run up by their mother.

Jennings could not be reached for comment.

This story is fictitious.

But how is it different from what we are actually doing to the next generation: spending trillions of dollars on infrastructure, health care, education, transportation, retirement, and "stimulative" pork, and charging it to the kids? Instead of being an act of fraud, however, the looting of the young has become bipartisan public policy. In 2011, 40 cents of every dollar the federal government spent was borrowed.

Even in an age of massive corporate bailouts, income transfers, and cash handouts, our ongoing intergenerational transfer of wealth is virtually unparalleled in history, inverting the normal relationship between generations. The Greatest Generation, quips former Wyoming senator Alan Simpson, has been replaced by the greediest generation, and we are leaving behind a legacy of generation-crushing, economy-wrecking debt.[1]

By 2020, the national debt will be more than the entire value of the national economy; interest payments on the debt alone will cost $1.1 trillion and will consume nearly half of all income tax revenue. But this is just the beginning: By 2050 the debt will be three times the Gross Domestic Product. In the next seventy years, the cost of interest alone will explode from 1.4 percent of GDP to more than 41 percent.[2]

The numbers are gravity bending: The unfunded obligations of Social Security are pegged at $7.7 trillion, but even this is dwarfed by Medicare's $37.9 trillion in unfunded liabilities. Entitlements (excluding net interest) account for 56 percent of all federal spending; by 2052 those entitlements (Medicare, Medicaid, and Social Security) will consume every last dollar of tax revenue.[3] Unless there is massive and politically painful reform, policymakers face the choice of eliminating every federal program except for the entitlements; raising taxes to confiscatory levels; or further increasing the debt to levels usually associated with the Third World.[4]

It's hard to imagine what America will look like by then. Citing numbers from the nonpartisan Congressional Budget Office, Congressmen Jeb Hensarling and Paul Ryan warn that when the national debt reaches 90 percent of GDP, "the needle is in the red zone and economic growth will begin to slow about one percent per year" or by about a third of the nation's projected economic growth. "The numbers are very, very clear," they write. "The publicly held debt exceeds the size of our economy in 2023. The CBO model that measures the economy basically crashes and breaks down in

2027 because it can't estimate what would actually happen to the economy if our debt levels get as high as they're projected to get."[5]

A Generation's Story

Because the numbers are so large and abstract, it helps to put them in more personal terms. Using Congressional Budget Office (CBO) projections we can get a picture of what life will be like for a child born in 2010.[6]

At birth, the child emerges from the womb owing about $29,178 as his or her share of the accumulated federal public debt.

By age 10, without spending a dime, every child's share of the nation's public debt will have risen by 70 percent to $49,694 per child.

In 2023, when they turn 13, their parents' generation will have stuck them with a bill for $58,971—double the debt they inherited at birth. According to the CBO, in 2023, for the first time, the per capita share of the debt will exceed the per capita Gross Domestic Product.

When the children turn 18 in 2028, their share of the national debt responsibility will have risen to $80,650.

Even if they have somehow managed to get through college debt-free, members of the class of 2032 will enter the workforce carrying a debt that has tripled in the last twenty-two years. They will attempt to launch their adult lives carrying a debt load of more than $103,800. As entitlement spending accelerates, so does their share of the debt.

By the time children born in 2010 turn 30, no matter how prudently they have managed their own finances, they will be saddled with a public debt of around $166,500, a burden that has risen 471 percent in three decades. The debt shadows their lives, choking out economic growth and stunting opportunity during what should be their most productive years.

At age 40, they will find themselves confronted with a public debt that will have grown from $9.1 trillion in 2010 to $122.8 trillion in 2050, an increase of 859 percent. In that year, each person's share of the national public debt will be $279,738. A family of four's share of the debt: $1.119 million.

Spend More, Borrow More, Worry Less

Even amidst the protestations of belated concern over the size of the debt, there have been influential voices on the left proclaiming: *Nothing to see here! No problem! All is well!*

Leading the charge for even more spending and borrowing was Nobel laureate Paul Krugman, who used his *New York Times* column to pooh-pooh concerns over rising deficits and to cheerlead for even more intergenerational transfers. Not only should the rising deficits not be seen as worrisome, Krugman insisted, "running big deficits in the face of the worst economic slump since the 1930s is actually the right thing to do." Leading a small band of progressives, Krugman urged President Obama and Congress to spend even more, faster, and damn the red ink: "If anything, deficits should be bigger than they are because the government should be doing more than it is to create jobs."

Krugman saved his greatest disdain for those who fretted about the trillion-dollar deficits. "Many economists," he wrote self-referentially, "take a much calmer view of budget deficits than anything you'll see on TV. . . . The long-run budget outlook is problematic, but short-term deficits aren't—and even the long-term outlook is much less frightening than the public is being led to believe." So upset was Krugman by the "deficit scare stories" and the "drumbeat of dire fiscal warnings" that the laureate resorted to a painfully strained analogy:

> To me—and I'm not alone in this—the sudden outbreak of deficit hysteria brings back memories of the groupthink that took hold during the run-up to the Iraq war. . . .
>
> Now, as then, those who challenge the prevailing narrative, no matter how strong their case and no matter how solid their background, are being marginalized.
>
> And fear-mongering on the deficit may end up doing as much harm as the fear-mongering on weapons of mass destruction.[7]

As absurd as it was to suggest that a Nobel Prize–winning columnist for *The New York Times* cheering on a Democratic president and Congress had somehow been "marginalized," Krugman's comparison to the run-up to the Iraq war was even more inapposite: Whereas the weapons of mass destruction may well have been nonexistent, the debt is all too real and unmistakable. The balance sheets of the government were littered with evidence of its destructive force. This is not a mirage.

Even so, Krugman dismissed concern over this as "deficit hysteria," declaring that "Washington now has its priorities all wrong: all the talk is about how to shave a few billion dollars off government spending, while there's hardly any willingness to tackle mass unemployment."

Underlying Krugman's case was the belief that deficits were effective in putting people back to work. But by early 2010, it had already become evident that the massive stimulus plan had failed to hold the line on unemployment. Supporters had promised that the massive deficit spending would hold the jobless rate to around 8 percent; but despite the gusher of borrowed cash, joblessness had neared 10 percent and even after the official end of the recession, the job market had continued to be weak despite attempts to spend and borrow our way to full employment. Faced with the demonstrable failure of the spending to deliver the results promised, Krugman's answer was to spend even more.

Krugman did make a brief, grudging acknowledgment that it was true that "there is a longer-term budget problem," and he admitted that even a full recovery "wouldn't balance the budget," and might not even reduce the deficit "to a permanently sustainable level." Someday, he admitted, the government might have to "increase its revenue and control its cost," but not now.[8] What his brief admission concealed was the scope of that problem: The fact is that entitlement spending was unsustainable long before the latest binge, which only served to accelerate the ongoing fiscal disaster.

Ironically, it was none other than Paul Krugman, circa 2003 (when George W. Bush was president), who had made that exact point. Indeed, Krugman (along with partisans on both sides of the divide) seems to take a somewhat relative view of deficits depending on who occupies the White House.

The same economist who dismissed worries over a 2009 deficit equal to 11 percent of GDP and a ten-year projection of $9 trillion sounded the alarm back in 2003 when Bush faced a deficit equal to 3 percent of GDP and a ten-year projected deficit of $1.8 trillion. In 2009 he shrugged off deficit fears, but in 2003 Krugman professed himself to be "terrified" and warned that the smaller Bush deficit was a "fiscal train wreck" and a "looming threat to the federal government's solvency."[9]

As the leading proponent of the Don't Sweat the Deficit movement, Krugman's own earlier deficit hysteria is worth quoting: "Last week," he declared back in March 2003, "I switched to a fixed-rate mortgage. It means higher monthly payments, but I'm terrified about what will happen to interest rates once financial markets wake up to the implications of skyrocketing budget deficits . . . we're looking at a fiscal crisis that will drive interest rates sky-high." Krugman continued:

> But what's really scary, what makes a fixed-rate mortgage seem like such a good idea, is the looming threat to the federal government's solvency.
>
> That may sound alarmist: right now the deficit, while huge in absolute terms, is only 2, make that 3, O.K., maybe 4 percent of G.D.P.
>
> But that misses the point . . . because of the future liabilities of Social Security and Medicare, the true budget picture is much worse than the conventional deficit numbers suggest. . . .
>
> How will the train wreck play itself out? . . . My prediction is that politicians will eventually be tempted to resolve the crisis the way irresponsible governments usually do: by printing money, both to pay current bills and to inflate away debt. And as that temptation becomes obvious, interest rates will soar.
>
> . . . investors still can't believe that the leaders of the United States are acting like the rulers of a banana republic. But I've done the math, and reached my own conclusions— and I've locked in my rate.[10]

Krugman may have locked in his rate, but apparently not his principles.

Dying in Debt

As Krugman backhandedly acknowledges, the exploding debt is being driven by four items: Social Security, Medicare, Medicaid, and net interest costs. Unlike discretionary spending that can be voted on by each Congress, these costs are largely on autopilot and are on target to swallow the federal budget.

The rising level of debt and the increasingly urgent warnings of a "super debt cycle" helped fuel the Republican resurgence of 2010, but Washington's fundamental unseriousness was exemplified by the appointment of a bipartisan deficit reduction commission whose recommendations were guaranteed to be ignored by both parties. (When politicians want to delay making a decision, they appoint a task force. When they want to avoid making a decision altogether, they name a Blue Ribbon task force or commission.) When George W. Bush called for reforming Social Security, warning that the system would collapse by 2042, Congress brushed him off. No changes were enacted. The doomsday date was still remote and the choices too painful to make in the near term. Politicians simply kicked the day of reckoning down the road to a later Congress and a later generation.

This brings us back to the ways that mooching changes both culture and character. For previous generations the idea of passing along massive debt to future generations was regarded as anathema, an act of not-just fiscal irresponsibility, but also dereliction of a moral duty. But decades of living off borrowed money has taken its toll on the American psyche, even among older Americans who were once known for their sense of financial probity. The extent to which the debt culture has changed the moral landscape was suggested by a survey by a firm called CESI Debt Solutions, which found that even retired senior citizens were running up credit-card debt for vacations or medical expenses, "and a surprising number have no intention of paying it off before they die." The survey found that as many as four out of ten retirees had added to their credit card debt "and aren't worried about paying it off in their lifetime." Some of them rationalize dying in debt as a way of sticking it to greedy banks. A vice president of CESI explained: "They think, 'Hey, I'm not going to pay back these guys who ripped off America.'"[11]In the end, of course, they will pass the debt along either to their children or to other consumers.

The Bank of Our Kids

In his comic novel *Boomsday*, Christopher Buckley imagines a revolt by the ripped-off young against a self-indulgent generation of boomers. The novel's heroine, Cassandra, finds that despite her years of study and admission to Yale, she is unable to afford college because her daddy has squandered her college fund; she enlists in the army instead. Cassandra's revenge comes a decade later when she uses her blog to foment generational revolution, complete with uprisings at golf courses where the white-haired geezers are living out their golden years at the expense of the debt-ridden members of Generation Whatever. The book's title refers to the day when millions of baby boomers begin to make the transition from taxpayers to tax receivers, or as Cassandra puts it pithily: "Mountainous debt, a deflating economy, and 77 million people retiring. The perfect economic storm." Ultimately her solution is, well, the ultimate solution: a system of "voluntary transitioning," which encourages the elderly to go quietly into the good night without bankrupting the country.[12] But no one is going quietly and the debt bomb isn't going away; we are too addicted to spending our children's money. Debt is, after all, the great enabler of spending.

Deficit spending makes every spending decision easier because it postpones hard choices and encourages politicians to do what they do best: spend Other People's Money without the other people figuring out that it is their money. At some level, everyone knows that there is no free money; even moochers know they are also the mooched upon. But no one wants to be a sucker, and even moochers can convince themselves they are somehow coming out ahead in the blizzard of criss-crossing dollars. Shifting the costs onto future generations is an essential part of the formula.

Would politicians be quite so ready to spend $60,000 an hour of tax money on Air Force One photo ops or $3.9 million rearranging office furniture at the Securities and Exchange Commission headquarters if they knew they would have to give the bill to living voters?[13] Would it be as easy for the government to spend $92 billion on corporate welfare, or $200 billion on lightly used and money-losing high-speed trains, if the bill was handed to taxpayers before the next election? In fact, high-speed trains are a perfect example of the allure of free money mooched from nonvoting future generations.

The Obama administration has already made a $10 billion down payment on a flashy plan to build "high-speed" rail corridors across the nation. All told, the price tag on the plan could reach $200 billion. "What would we get for this huge investment?" asks economist Robert Samuelson. "Not much. Here's what we wouldn't get: any meaningful reduction in traffic congestion, greenhouse-gas emissions, air travel, or oil consumption and imports. *Nada, zip.*" Even though it has somehow "become fashionable to think that high-speed trains" will help save the planet, Samuelson notes: "They won't. They're a perfect example of wasteful spending masquerading as a respectable social cause."[14]

But across the country the argument for the trains essentially boils down to: Take the money or someone else will. States are pitted against states and cities against cities; they're encouraged to compete with one another for a chance to spend money we don't have on projects we don't need. None of that would be possible without the ability to shift the cost onto future generations.

This is true across the board.

Between 2000 and 2010, overall federal spending grew 62 percent faster than inflation. Discretionary spending rose 79 percent faster than inflation; antipoverty spending rose 89 percent faster than inflation. Since 2000, Medicaid and food stamp rolls have exploded with costs and benefits also exceeding inflation. Under the Bush administration, federal spending increased to 20.9 percent of GDP. Even as the recession took hold, the government revved up its spending to a post-WWII record of 24.7 percent of GDP. Officials project a slight dip, but then a surge of spending to 26.5 percent of GDP by 2020.[15]

The only way this is possible is to charge it to the Bank of the Kids.

Optimists have suggested that the next generation can avoid fiscal Armageddon by simply growing the economy. But while the economy, as measured by the GDP, is estimated to grow by $34,258 per person in the next forty years, the public debt will grow by more than $250,000 per capita.[16] We can't grow ourselves out of this one.

Where will the money have gone? We'll have spent it on shiny new trains, on farm subsidies and television converter boxes, corporate bailouts and our retirements and health care. Think of it as the Mother of all Mooches.

Part Six

WHAT'S FAIR?

An Abbreviated History of Mooching

☆ ☆ ☆

Late in the day a farmer is harvesting his crop, which he uses to feed his family. He takes the surplus to market to sell it to neighbors, who use it to feed their families.* The farmer uses the profits to expand his house and buy a new plow from the blacksmith, who in turn has more money for bread and even enough left over to send his daughter to school.

Or would, if not for the moochers, whose approach has evolved over time.

Early Moochers: Four large hairy brigands ride up and threaten the farmer with clubs unless he gives them his crops. He complies but is beaten anyway. They steal his goat.

Feudal Moocher. The lord of the manor rides up and demands that the farmer give him 80 percent of the crop. The farmer complies and sends along his daughter for good measure.

Modern Moochers: Four enlightened and compassionate officials drive up in an environmentally friendly vehicle.

They greet the farmer and then explain their concern over the gap between food "haves" and "have nots." The farmer tries to explain that he is helping to fix the problem by growing more food, which he intends to take to market to sell to the "have nots."

---

* In this particular tale, the farmer does not benefit from any of the agricultural subsidies described in earlier chapters.

But, his visitors suggest, shouldn't his crop be distributed on the basis of "needs" and "fairness"? The word "greed" is frequently used.

Perhaps the farmer doesn't realize, suggests one of his visitors, how bad this is for the self-esteem of those who do not own land; or how unfair his bountiful harvest seems for those who for a rather long list of reasons choose not to plant their land the way the farmer does. There are frequent references to children who will go hungry if the farmer keeps the crops for his own use or insists on selling it at a "profit."

The farmer points out that his expanding crop actually makes food cheaper and that he voluntarily sets aside a portion for the indigent, but his visitors suggest that the crop should rightfully be distributed on the basis of "justice," rather than charity.

Somewhat annoyed by now, the farmer asks what is "just" about taking away the crops that he has planted, tended, and now harvested?

They assure him that they are not proposing to steal his crop, but merely to help him "spread the wealth around" a little through a "fairness" tax or fee.

One of the visitors, apparently a tenured academic of some sort, suggests that he should hardly take credit for what is obviously brute luck. His hard work, he explains, is simply an accident of genetics and background for which he deserves no credit. Wouldn't it therefore be more equitable to simply divide up the produce among all of the villagers?

As evening turns into night, someone proposes they vote democratically, and after several ballots, the visitors vote themselves shares of the man's crop. Only when they are done dividing the spoils do they notice that the farmer has disappeared.

Chapter 18

WE'RE ALL FROM STARNESVILLE NOW

So what is fair? What do we owe one another and what right or claim do we have on our own wealth and that of others? What is the tipping point between a compassionate society and a nation of moochers?

More to the point: What does justice demand? Leaving aside the cost, isn't it both more just and fair for a society to spread the wealth around, to redistribute it from the "privileged" to the "underprivileged" based on need?

In *Atlas Shrugged*, Ayn Rand offers an answer in the form of a morality play of her own devising, set in a town called Starnesville, Wisconsin.[1]

Rand's story of the Twentieth Century Motor Company has a central place in the novel (spoiler alert). It marks the beginning of John Galt's mission, while also describing in miniature what Galt stands against and why he felt compelled to stop the motor of the world. Rand tries to show the fundamental immorality behind the moral "ideal" of "from each according to his ability, to each according to his needs." Far from being a moral ideal that lacked something of practicality, Rand insisted that a needs-based society is a truly hellacious idea, the stuff of nightmares that turns honest men into dishonest ones. In a brutal transvaluation of values, a horrible idea had somehow been elevated into a moral precept.

The "Family"

In the book, the owner of the Twentieth Century Motor Company dies and leaves the thriving enterprise to his three children, Eric, Gerald, and Ivy Starnes, who have very different ideas than their father on how to run the business. They call together all of the employees for a meeting at which they vote to adopt a plan that "everybody in the factory would work according to his ability, but would be paid according to his need."[2] The narrator explains the reasons for the vote: Everyone assumed that they would have the edge over someone who was better off, forgetting all of those less able than they were, who would also get unearned benefits at their expense.

At first the whole group voted on needs. "It took us just one meeting to discover that we had become beggars—rotten, whining, sniveling beggars, all of us, because no man could claim his pay as his rightful earnings . . . so he had to beg in public for relief for his needs, like any lousy moocher. . . ."[3] The competition was no longer who could work hardest, or most creatively, or most productively: "it turned into a contest among six thousand panhandlers, each claiming that *his* need was worse than his brother's."[4]

The employees were introduced to the Sucker Principle: "Your honesty was like a tool left at the mercy of the next man's dishonesty. The honest ones paid, the dishonest collected."[5]

Needs turned out to be endless, while ability became a liability. The ablest men were required to work longer hours and nights— taxed—to support the ever growing neediness of others who had figured out how the system really worked.

A young man afire with ideas and ambition was foolish enough to come up with ideas to save thousands of man hours, but he found himself voted one of the "ablest" and "sentenced to night work." The flow of ideas stopped: He had learned his lesson.

As Ivy Starnes later explains: "Rewards were based on need, and penalties on ability."[6]

The Starnes

In this morality play, the Starnes family is a triptych of villainy, with each of the siblings a different type of moocher advocacy.

Eric Starnes craves popularity, a glad hander who is obsessed with being liked. "He wanted to be loved, it seems," says a former worker. "We couldn't stand him."[7]

Gerald Starnes is in it for the glory and the cash; he milks the system, surrounding himself with magazine covers touting his benevolence, which he makes as conspicuous as his own greed, "flashing diamond cuff links the size of a nickel and shaking cigar ashes all over," while claiming that the lushness of his lifestyle was not for himself, but for the benefit of the company and its noble plan. The employees hated him.[8]

But the most dangerous was Ivy, the ideological purist, who

illustrates how the enforcement of "fairness" morphs into the exercise of arbitrary power. Ivy is not motivated by popularity or celebrity, but rather by "goodness," which translates into power.

Unlike her brothers, she didn't care about material wealth. She dressed in "scuffed, flat-heeled shoes and shirtwaists—just to show how selfless she was." Ivy was Director of Distribution. "She was the one who held us by the throat."[9]

The dramatic heart of the chapter is the story of an "old guy" who loved phonograph records. A childless widower, he had gone so far as to skip meals so he could afford to buy more classical music, his only real pleasure. But under the new regime, his solitary enjoyment was not considered a sufficient "need" to justify an allowance for what they deemed a "personal luxury." At the same meeting a girl described as a "mean, ugly little eight-year-old" was voted gold braces for her buck teeth because the company psychologist worried that her self-esteen might be damaged unless her teeth were straightened. The man who loved music turned to drink and one night as he staggered down the street, he saw the girl with the gold braces and "swung his fist and knocked all her teeth out. Every one of them."[10]

Let's cut Rand some slack and assume that she was not endorsing the music lover's attack on the buck-toothed child; rather she used its violence to dramatize how characters were warped, distorted, and ultimately destroyed by the "plan." Despite the unctuous good intentions, basing a society on "need" did not result in a kinder or gentler society.

The story of the collapse of Twentieth Century Motors has one final twist: a character named Eugene Lawson, the "banker with a heart," whose bad loans cause his bank to fail and destroy the local Wisconsin economy. His first words in the book are: "I am not ashamed of it."[11] Despite the economic devastation his actions wrought, Lawson's self-esteem is intact and he remains convinced of his moral superiority.

Lawson is a precursor of more modern bankers who handed out

money based on "need," rather than sound finances. His motives, he assures us, "were pure," even though everything he touched turned to failure and ruin.[12] Oddly enough, not even Ayn Rand could envision a world in which the Eugene Lawsons would be bailed out by taxpayers.

A final irony: After crashing the bank and spreading economic devastation in his wake, Lawson ends up as a high-ranking government bureaucrat.

Chapter 19

WHAT'S FAIR?

What is the answer to the ideologies of redistribution?

Our answer has to start with the principle that individuals have a legitimate claim to their own incomes and that their wealth is not simply held at the sufferance of the political class.

Robert Nozick noted that any form of compulsory income redistribution is a serious matter, as it involves "the violation of people's rights." For Nozick, taxation on wages was "on a par with forced labor . . . Seizing the results of someone's labor is equivalent to seizing hours from him and directing him to carry on various activities." In effect, argued Nozick, if someone forces you to do uncompensated work they become a "part-owner of you."

"The result," he concluded, "is a shift from the classical liberal's notion of self-ownership to the notion of (partial) property rights in *other* people."[1]

Enforcing an arbitrary standard of equality or "fairness" on society or individuals cannot be maintained "without continuous interference with people's lives." To maintain a pattern of "fair" distribution of wealth (however that is defined by the political elites of the moment), Nozick wrote, means that "one must either continually interfere to stop people from transferring resources as they wish to, or continually (or periodically) interfere to take from some persons resources that others for some reason chose to transfer to them."[2] In other words, people will continue to make decisions that will result in some people getting more and others less, regardless of how it affects the preferred "pattern" of income distribution.

In a free economy, for example, people will freely give money to the man who builds the most efficient engines, or to the basketball player (Nozick famously used the example of Wilt Chamberlain, but LeBron James or Kobe Bryant would work just as well) who displays the most talent and skill. Those individual choices may result in inequalities of wealth that can only be fixed by substituting government action for the choices freely made.[3]

Nozick's alternative to the standard "from each according to his ability to each according to his needs" was "From each as they choose, to each as they are chosen [in free, voluntary, and just exchanges]."[4]

What Do We Deserve?

But do we really deserve the rewards we get? Or are we being greedy by insisting that we have a greater claim on our income than those who stake a claim to it on the basis of their "need"?

The notion that wealth is the result of effort rather than mere luck has been under intellectual siege for decades. Whether they are conscious of it or not, many advocates of income transfers draw their inspiration not from Marx, but from John Rawls, who argued that society should maximize the position of the least well off.

Despite his influence on modern liberal thinking, few candidates for elective office are likely to cite Rawls in their stump speeches. As William Voegeli notes, "People who call themselves Rawlsians, however, are always candidates for the faculty senate, not the US Senate."[5] But thinkers like Rawls provide the intellectual architecture for much of modern progressivism; and even if they are unseen, they are like the poets whom Percy Bysshe Shelley declared to be the "unacknowledged legislators of the world." Behind every welfare program of the last half century there is a Rawlsian, whether he knows it or not.

Rawls's contribution is twofold: He provides the intellectual heft behind the argument that we should measure the virtue and justness of society by the extent of its redistribution of wealth. He also undermines the idea that rewards should be based on individual merit by suggesting that most of our advantages are matters of chance for which we deserve no credit. This includes our natural talents, which he regards as "morally arbitrary" and which should not influence the distribution of things like opportunities, income, wealth, and "the social bases of self-respect."

Our natural qualities, argues Rawls, are decided "by the outcome of the natural lottery; and this outcome is arbitrary from a moral perspective. There is no more reason to permit the distribution of income and wealth to be settled by the distribution of natural assets than by historical and social fortune."[6]

What then about character? Some will make the most of their natural gifts, but some will squander them. Natural talent alone does not equal success, as many would-be celebrities demonstrate on a regular basis. And what about the effort expended to make the most of those natural gifts? Rawls dismisses both character and effort.

"The assertion that a man deserves the superior character that enables him to make the effort to cultivate his abilities is equally problematic," writes Rawls, "for his character depends in large part upon fortunate family and social circumstances for which he can claim no credit."[7] If he can claim no credit, it follows that he has at best a limited claim to the rewards.

Language has played a crucial role in advancing this notion that success and achievement are arbitrary and largely a result of chance and good luck. Consider all of the euphemisms that describe successful individuals as "fortunate," "privileged," or simply, "the haves." The nomenclature is specifically designed to diminish the sense of deserving of those who are better off by blurring any recognition that their status might be a reward for achievement, innovation, risk taking, or hard work.

Admittedly the term "privileged" might fairly describe a third-generation heir or Hollywood celebrity frittering away their life on the island of Ibiza, but it distorts the reality of much of how wealth is created. Even the entrepreneur from a good family and other "morally arbitrary" natural advantages lives with the very real possibility that everything he has worked for will be lost; that the bank will call in his note, crushing his ability to make a payroll; or that a tax hike or new regulation will erase his narrow margin of profitability. In what sense, after all, is a small businessman who runs a start-up metal fabrication company "privileged"? By carrying the risk? The debt? By submitting his livelihood and family income to the vagaries of the marketplace and competition?

But this is precisely why the insistence that inequality is "morally arbitrary" is crucial to the politics of redistribution of income. There would be a very different tenor to the debate over "spreading around the wealth" if we substituted the words "achievers," "doers," and "makers," for "the fortunate," "the privileged," and "the haves." Language matters: It is not a coincidence that progressives have taken to calling the recipients of government aid the "less fortunate," the "underprivileged," and "victims." Language shapes the debate when an advocate says that "we should raise taxes so the privileged can share their good fortune with the underprivileged."

Imagine instead if a politician made his or her case this way: "We need to raise taxes so that achievers are forced to share their rewards with society's moochers."

The Content of Our Character

This is not, however, the worst. Rawls's denial that we deserve to be rewarded for our personal characteristics ultimately robs us of individuality; in search of a theory of "fairness," we lose our personhood. In a critique of Rawls, David Schmidtz addresses Rawls's claim that we can't give an individual credit for being a person of good character. "Jane's character is not something that happened to her," writes Schmidtz. "*It is her.*" (Emphasis in original.) "Thus, if we say exemplary character is morally arbitrary, it is people not merely character that we are refusing to take seriously." Giving people credit for what they achieve and what they are "is the essence of treating them as persons rather than as mere confluences of historical forces."[8]

Thus, notes Schmidtz, when we say Martin Luther King, Jr., spoke of a time when his children would be judged by the "content of their character," he presumably was not envisioning a time when the nation would regard their characters as "accidents for which they could claim no credit."[9]

Nor would such a world be fairer or more just. If we accept that we have no inherent right to the income or property we have justly and fairly acquired because our success is the result of random historical and social chance, who decides what we deserve? Congress? Philosopher kings? Or Ivy Starnes?

This brings us back to Rawls, who argues that society should maximize the position of the least well off. Rawls is a complex thinker and I won't attempt to deal with all of the interpretations and variations on his philosophy, except to point out that it is a non sequitur to argue that arranging a society to the best advantage of the poor is advanced by the welfare state.

What if it turns out that income redistribution creates economic and social conditions that make the poor less well off?

The Miracle of the Private

Life in the West is not merely easier than it was two centuries ago, it is exponentially better; the quality of our housing, diets, and medical care have all improved so dramatically that the scope of the transformation is sometimes hard to grasp. In economically developed countries, income per capita is 1,600 percent of what it was two hundred years ago. It is, Rich Lowry notes, the "miracle of the modern world."[10]

At the beginning of the nineteenth century all but the wealthy lived virtually a subsistence existence. "The average human consumed and expected her children and grandchildren and great-grandchildren to go on consuming a mere $3 a day," writes historian Deirdre N. McCloskey. "It had been this way for all of history, and for that matter all of prehistory. With her $3 a day the average denizen of the earth got a few pounds of potatoes, a little milk, an occasional scrap of meat."[11] Much of the world remains that way.

What changed for countries like ours was not a regime of confiscation and redistribution (although that was tried), but the unleashing of the creative energies of individuals and enterprises who sought a better future through work, production, trade, and enterprise. They flourished as long as those qualities were rewarded and encouraged to thrive rather than regarded with suspicion or seen as milch cows for schemes of social improvement.

Oddly enough, this has been a lesson learned, unlearned, and relearned throughout history. The concept of the "tragedy of the commons," for instance, goes back to Aristotle, who noticed a basic human trait: "For that which is common to the greatest number has the least care bestowed upon it."

If responsibility is diffused among many, it is always someone else's problem. Aristotle understood the dynamic, familiar to every communal enterprise: "Everyone thinks chiefly of his own, hardly at all of the common interest; and only when he is himself concerned as an individual. For besides other considerations, everybody is more inclined to neglect the duty which he expects another to fulfill. . . ."[12]

Unfortunately, the lesson has been lost on two millennia of social planners, who continue to be baffled by the (completely predictable) failure of their well-intentioned collective schemes.

But the flip side is just as important: When the collective farm is privatized, when individuals are left free to pursue their own prosperity, remarkable things happen. People begin to work harder, more creatively, faster, smarter, and the entire community is enriched. If what Aristotle described is the "tragedy of the commons," the reverse ought to be recognized as the "miracle of the private."

There will continue, of course, to be pockets of poverty and there will always be those who may through no fault of their own not be able to participate, but it is precisely because of the shift of responsibility and reward to the individual that we can create the surplus wealth that has made the condition of the poor in the United States so markedly better than the life experienced by the poor throughout much of the developing world.

As the experiment of the last sixty years ought to have made abundantly clear, the transfer of cash can have quite the opposite effect by distorting incentives, undermining the culture, breaking up families, and destroying neighborhoods. Despite spending trillions of dollars we still have vast swaths of dysfunction and dependency, especially in central cities. This suggests that simply expanding the welfare state does not solve the problem of poverty; that increased dependency has not worked to help the poor as much as it has helped advocates feel better about themselves. Far from bettering the condition of society's least well off, redistribution can actually worsen their lives and dim their future prospects.

Why?

Policies that expand or encourage more dependence do not better the conditions of the poor because they undermine the conditions that hold the most promise of economic advancement and personal fulfillment. Poverty cannot be solved simply by providing more money because poverty is not simply a matter of dollars and cents: It is also a product of culture, spirit, and character. Treating poverty as simply a matter of economics runs the risk of cash transfers that destroy the very values and incentives that provide the best hope for the poor to get out of poverty.

If a main cause of poverty is lack of jobs, then a society should be structured to provide the maximum opportunities and protections for the poor to obtain those jobs. Conversely, policies that slow the creation of such opportunities—no matter how compassionately meant—do not ultimately help the poor.

If another cause of poverty is poor education, we ought to create an environment where the needs of poor children are paramount, as opposed to the entrenched special interests of public education who have used the rhetoric of caring about kids to fatten their own wallets.

If another cause of childhood poverty is family breakdown and illegitimacy, we should avoid policies like Aid to Families with Dependent Children, which encouraged the departure of male breadwinners and incentivized out-of-wedlock births. Policies that render the male breadwinner unnecessary because the state has replaced him with a handout do not make life better for the children who will grow up fatherless; programs that make dependency more attractive than getting a job do not create a culture conducive to the advancement of the poor to self-sufficiency.

Massive debt and excessive taxation (and perverse incentives in transfer payments) can punish extra work, while a stagnant economy, high joblessness, and high interest rates can slow or even block social and economic mobility.

Finally, we need to recognize that mooching simply recycles wealth; it does not generate it. Increasing wealth requires the initiative, innovation, and willingness to work and take risks that are often incompatible with a culture that encourages taking one's ease at the trough instead.

Chapter 20

STEP AWAY FROM THE TROUGH

How do we begin to dismantle Moocher Nation? How can we encourage Americans to back away from the trough at a time when it seems overflowing with a cornucopia of benefits, credits, pork, and perks, all paid for by others?

The challenge is both political and cultural. Real change requires a transformation of the habit and expectation of dependency. By "blackening the skies with criss-crossing dollars" (to use William Voegeli's memorable phrase), the moocher state has encouraged even normally independent Americans to line up for their slice, lest they be left out. In a transfer-spending state, individuals rationalize their own dip at the trough by saying to themselves that they are simply getting back some of what they have paid in, and since everyone else is feeding freely it would be foolish not to partake as well.

Retired philosophy professor Kelly L. Ross compares the dynamic to the classic "prisoner's dilemma," in which two prisoners planning an escape have to decide whether to keep the secret (and thus jointly benefit from a dash to freedom), or betray the other (and thereby win a reward from the jailers). The basic idea is that if you are a prisoner planning to escape with some fellow prisoners, you have the choice of being faithful to them and benefiting from their plan, or you can betray them and earn what may be a very considerable reward from the authorities. In either case, players of the "game" have to consider whether the other prisoner might betray them first, bringing down a world of woe on his fellow trusting prisoner.

Ross notes that there is a similar moocher dilemma. Even if it becomes obvious that "not everyone can live off of the wealth of everyone else," and even though it is clear that everyone would be better off if everyone left off seeking to loot others, "it is obvious that the best course for each individual group is to get everyone else to give up rent-seeking [read privileges, special benefits, pork] while they alone covertly continue to collect" their share of the goodies.[1]

He explains:

> The fear that others will pursue such a strategy is easily sufficient motivation not to give up rent-seeking [mooching]. No one, of course, blatantly advertises their rent-seeking in terms of their own self-interest. Instead, there are always high sounding, moralistic slogans and rationalizations, arguments that special benefits are necessary because of poverty, compassion, discrimination, racism, the environment, greedy insurance companies, greedy businessmen, etc.

But they are all ultimately claims to government-granted perks, privileges, or simply other people's cash.

All Together

This suggests that an assault on the moocher culture will require a more or less simultaneous backing away from the trough. No one wants to go first.

Farmers might be more willing to tolerate a loss of their bloated subsidies if they knew that others were making similar sacrifices; corporate welfare is easier to choke off if companies realize that they are not alone in having to shift for themselves. Similarly, the middle class is more likely to accept losses of credits and handouts if they believe that others are also making similar sacrifices.

This may seem somewhat counterintuitive. Practically speaking, incremental changes that chip away at the spending culture seem more realistic; but because of the nature of the moocher state it might be easier to sell a shared return to personal responsibility.

The Cato Institute estimates that the federal government operates more than two thousand separate subsidy programs—fully twice as many as existed in the mid-1980s. This blizzard of crisscrossing dollars includes farm subsidies, entitlements, school lunches and breakfasts, food stamps, housing assistance, corporate welfare, student loans, and health care spending.

As Cato notes: "Each subsidy program costs money, generates a bureaucracy, spawns lobby groups, and encourages more people to demand freebies from the government. Individuals, businesses, and nonprofit groups that become hooked on federal subsidies essentially become tools of the state. They lose their independence, they have less incentive to innovate, and they shy away from criticizing the government."[2]

What would a reform program look like? It would have to be far-reaching, tightening food stamp eligibility and turning off the money taps to corporate America; eliminating middle-class handouts and tax credits while simultaneously cutting unnecessary pork and bloated public employee pensions; and dialing back the entitlement culture by moving Medicare and Social Security to more sustainable systems. (Congressman Paul Ryan's "Roadmap" would be a good starting place.)[3]

But most of all, the revolution against Moocherism requires redefining our expectations of what others owe to us and what we owe ourselves. Put bluntly, we need to restore some of the stigma to mooching. Our capacity for rationalization has proven to be quite remarkable, but at some level, most Americans retain a lingering sense that there's something wrong about feeding at the trough, even if everyone else is doing it. That instinct needs to be reinforced, which is no small task amidst the blizzard of handouts and giveaways.

We should start with discussions of language (bringing back the word "mooch" is a good start, I think) and move to questions of personal and national character.

What kind of a people do we want to be? Dependents who play the endless shell game of living off what others produce, or a society that values and encourages independence and self-sufficiency?

Like the overuse of the "victim card," Moocherism has also exacted a heavy tax on our compassion. Americans remain an extraordinarily compassionate people, but it is difficult to escape the sense that we are suffering from compassion fatigue. Despite the rhetoric deployed to rationalize giveaways, we have not become a kinder, gentler, or more compassionate society. Rather, the flight from personal responsibility and the culture of infinite entitlement have generated skepticism about the very idea that we have moral obligations to the less fortunate. The gridlock of national politics, the growing polarization between right and left, and the refusal of interest groups to give up any of their demands for the public good—all are symptoms of the "What's in it for me?" mentality that fuels Moocher Nation. Recall Mancur Olson's observation that the "gang fight is fully as rough as the individual duel, and the struggle of special interest groups generates no magnanimity or altruism. . . . Competition about the division of income is not any nicer than competition to produce or to please customers."[4]

Needs and Wants

There are, of course, people with real needs: The elderly and the disabled have special needs and society has an ongoing obligation to lend them a hand. But here is the rub: There has been a purposeful muddling of genuine need and things that we merely want. They are not at all the same thing, and the first thing we have to do is separate the social safety net from the squishy pillow of, for example, taxpayer-provided electric cars.

A revolution against Moocherism requires hard-headed distinctions between actual needs and things we want. For decades now, as George Lightbourn, president of the Wisconsin Policy Research Institute, notes, "Our leaders surmised that if they did not swaddle every ugly problem in the comforting blanket of government, they had failed."[5]

Instead, politicians will have to learn to say no—even to ideas that might seem attractive. Equally as important, so will the rest of us, even if the public trough seems both convenient and desirable.

The assault on the moocher culture is not a rejection of compassion, but it does require a redefinition of what we mean by a compassionate society.

A Compassionate Society

A compassionate society makes sure that people do not starve. It does not buy free lunch for everyone.

A compassionate society makes provisions so that the homeless or the otherwise destitute are not exposed to the elements. It does not provide no-down-payment, no-income loans so that people can buy unaffordable houses at inflated prices.

A compassionate society provides opportunities; it does not treat free cell phones or wireless Internet as an entitlement. It does not punish work or make it easier to be dependent than it is to get a job and improve yourself.

A compassionate society provides the opportunity and the freedom to travel. It does not compel you to buy your neighbor a new car.

A compassionate society provides a temporary safety net for the unlucky. It does not provide a soft mattress for a lifetime of dependency.

A compassionate society may cushion the worst effect of the business cycles. It does not provide billion-dollar bailouts to the business whose reckless bets go south.

A compassionate society takes care of those in need. It does not assume that we are all incapable of making it on our own.

A compassionate society does not infantilize its citizens or corrupt them by making them a nation of moochers.

Notes

Preface

1. P. J. O'Rourke, "A Nation of Moochers: Happy April 15," *The Weekly Standard*, April 13, 2009.

2. William Baldwin, "What's Your State's Moocher Ratio?" *Forbes* magazine, November 30, 2009.

Scenes from Moocher Nation

1. Joe Hagan, "Tenacious G, Inside Goldman Sachs, America's Most Successful, Cynical, Envied, Despised, and (in Its View, Anyway) Misunderstood Engine of Capitalism," *New York* magazine, July 26, 2009.

2. Craig Schneider and Tammy Joyner, "Housing Crisis Reaches Full Boil in East Point; 62 Injured," *Atlanta Journal-Constitution*, August 11, 2010.

3. *The Foundry*, "Morning Bell: End Crony Capitalism," the Heritage Foundation, August 18, 2010.

4. *Los Angeles Times*, "Millions in California Welfare Money Spent at Vacation Playgrounds," October 3, 2010.

5. Thomas Frank, "Huge Losses Put Federal Flood Insurance Plan in the Red," *USA Today*, August 26, 2010.

6. Associated Press, "Feds Wasted Millions in Utilities Program for Poor," July 1, 2010.

7. Dan Morgan, Gilbert M. Gaul, and Sarah Cohen, "Farm Program Pays $1.3 Billion to People Who Don't Farm," *Washington Post*, July 2, 2006.

Chapter 1. A Nation of Moochers

1. Scott A. Hodge, "Once Self-Reliant, Now a Nation of Takers," *Investor's Business Daily,* April 7, 2010.

2. David Schmidtz, *Elements of Justice* (New York: Cambridge University Press, 2006), 11.

3. Jeanne Sahadi, "47% Will Pay No Federal Income Tax: An Increasing Number of Households End Up Owing Nothing in Major Federal Taxes, but the Situation May Not Be Sustainable over the Long Run," *CNNMoney.com,* October 3, 2009, http://money.cnn.com/2009/09/30/pf/taxes/who_pays_taxes/index.htm.

4. Stephen Ohlemacher, "Nearly Half of U.S. Households Escape Fed Income Tax," Associated Press, April 7, 2010.

5. Hodge, "Once Self-Reliant."

6. Stephen Moore, "We've Become a Nation of Takers, Not Makers," *Wall Street Journal,* April 1, 2011.

7. Richard Wolf, "Record Number in Government Anti-poverty Programs," *USA Today,* August 30, 2010.

8. William W. Beach and Patrick D. Tyrell, "The 2010 Index of Dependence on Government," Center for Data Analysis, The Heritage Foundation, October 14, 2010.

9. Ibid.

10. Janet Novack and Stephanie Fitch, "When Work Doesn't Pay for the Middle Class," *Forbes,* October 5, 2009.

11. Brent T. White, "Underwater and Not Walking Away: Shame, Fear and the Social Management of the Housing Crisis," *Arizona Legal Studies,* Discussion Paper No. 09-35, October 2009.

12. James R. Hagerty and Nick Timiraos, "Debtor's Dilemma: Pay the Mortgage or Walk Away," *Wall Street Journal,* December 17, 2009.

13. Dennis Cauchon, "Federal Workers Earning Double Their Private Counterparts," *USA Today,* August 13, 2010.

14. Jason DeParle and Robert Gebeloff, "Food Stamp Use Soars, and Stigma Fades," *New York Times,* November 28, 2009.

15. *Wall Street Journal,* "In U.S., 14% Rely on Food Stamps," November 4, 2010.

16. Lindsey Tanner, "Food Stamps Will Feed Half of US Kids, Study Says," Associated Press, November 2, 2009.

17. Dennis Cauchon, "Private Pay Shrinks to Historic Lows as Gov't Payouts Rise," *USA Today,* May 26, 2010.

18. Beach and Tyrell, "The 2010 Index."

19. Brian Riedl, "Federal Spending by the Numbers 2010," The Heritage Foundation, Special Report #78, June 1, 2010.

20. Ibid.

21. Projections were calculated by the Heritage Foundation using Congressional Budget Office, "The Budget and Economic Outlook: An Update," August 2010, http://www.cbo.gov/ftpdocs/117xx/doc11705/08-18-Update.pdf.

22. William Voegeli, *Never Enough, America's Limitless Welfare State* (New York: Encounter Books, 2010), 7.

Chapter 2. Have We Reached the Tipping Point?

1. Rep. Paul Ryan, "Should America Bid Farewell to Exceptional Freedom?" *Real Clear Politics,* April 2, 2010. Congressman Paul Ryan delivered this speech to the Oklahoma Council of Public Affairs in Oklahoma City on March 31, 2010.

2. Mancur Olson, *The Rise and Decline of Nations* (New Haven: Yale University Press, 1982), 72.

3. Frederic Bastiat, *The Law,* trans. Dean Russell (Irvington-on-Hudson, N.Y.: Foundation for Economic Education, 1998), 6–8.

4. Thomas Byrne Edsall, "The Obama Coalition," *The Atlantic,* April 2010.

Chapter 3. The Rise of Moocher Nation

1. Heather Mac Donald, "The Sidewalks of San Francisco: Can the City by the Bay Reclaim Public Space from Aggressive Vagrants?" *The City Journal,* Autumn 2010.

2. Fred Siegel, *The Future Once Happened Here* (New York: The Free Press, 1997), 61.

3. Ibid.

4. MacDonald, "The Sidewalks."

5. Ibid.

6. Ibid.

7. Myron Magnet, *The Dream and the Nightmare* (New York: Encounter Books, 1993), 1.

8. Siegel, *The Future*, 10

9. Gareth Davies, *From Opportunity to Entitlement: The Transformation and Decline of Great Society Liberalism* (Lawrence, Kan.: University Press of Kansas, 1996), 3.

10. James Coleman, "Self-Suppression of Academic Freedom," Address to the National Association of Scholars, New York, June 19, 1990.

11. Davies, *From Opportunity*, 9.

12. Ibid., 6.

13. Siegel, *The Future*, 57.

14. Ibid., 59.

15. Ibid.

16. Ibid.

17. Daniel Patrick Moynihan, "The Negro Family: The Case for National Action," Washington, D.C.: U.S. Department of Labor, 1965.

18. William Ryan, *Blaming the Victim* (New York: Vintage Books, 1971), 122.

19. Lawrence Medd, "From Here to Intolerance," *The Economist*, July 20, 1991.

20. Ryan, *Blaming the Victim*, 25

21. Charles J. Sykes, *A Nation of Victims* (New York: St. Martin's Press, 1992), 109.

22. Quoted in Siegel, *The Future*, 50–51.

23. Ibid., 51.

24. Ibid., 60.

25. Ibid.

26. Davies, *From Opportunity*, 229.

27. Siegel, *The Future*, 52.

28. Quoted in Davies, *From Opportunity*, 118; Nick Kotz and Mary Ann Kotz, *A Passion for Equality* (New York: Norton, 1970), 183.

29. Quoted in Siegel, *The Future*, 53.

30. Davies, *From Opportunity*, 235.

Chapter 4. The Joys of Dependency

1. Roy Mark, "Feds Tapped Out of DTV Coupons," *Eweek.com*, January 6, 2009, http://www.eweek.com/c/a/Government-IT/Feds-Tapped-Out-of-DTV-Coupons.

2. Paul Sims, "Why Work When I Can Get £42,000 in Benefits a Year AND Drive a Mercedes?" *Daily Mail*, April 13, 2010.

3. Anis Shivani, "New Rules for Writers: Ignore Publicity, Shun Crowds, Refuse Recognition and More," *Huffington Post*, January 16, 2011, http://www.huffingtonpost.com/anis-shivani/new-rules-for-writers_b_808558.html.

4. Vivian Ho, "Obama's Aunt Says 'System' Was at Fault," *Boston Globe*, September 21, 2010.

5. Robert Rector, "How Poor Are America's Poor? Examining the 'Plague' of Poverty in America," The Heritage Foundation, August 27, 2007.

6. Ibid.

7. Thomas Sowell, *Economic Facts and Fallacies* (New York: Basic Books, 2008), 129.

8. Ibid.

9. Ibid., 128.

10. Matt Richtel, "Providing Cellphones for the Poor," *New York Times*, June 14, 2009.

11. Alfred Lubrano, "Advocates Say Poor Need Available Free Cell Phones," *Philadelphia Inquirer*, June 14, 2010.

12. R. S. McCain, "Free Cellphones for the Poor!" *TheOtherMcCain.com*, October 9, 2008, http://rsmccain.blogspot.com/2008/10/free-cellphones-for-poor.html.

13. Kiki Bradley and Robert Rector, "Confronting the Unsustainable Growth of Welfare Entitlements, Principles of Reform and the Next Steps," The Heritage Foundation, Backgrounder #2427, June 24, 2010.

14. Siegel, *The Future*, 46.

15. Voegeli, *Never Enough*, 9.

16. Kiki Bradley, "Expanding the Failed War on Poverty: Obama's 2011 Budget Increases Welfare Spending to Historic Levels," the Heritage Foundation, WebMemo #2838, March 21, 2010.

17. Ibid.

18. Beach and Tyrell, "The 2010 Index."

19. Bradley and Rector, "Confronting the Unsustainable Growth."

20. Ibid.

21. John Cassidy, "Relatively Deprived: How Poor Is Poor?" *New Yorker*, April 3, 2006.

22. Schmidtz, *Elements of Justice*, 118.

The Kindness of Strangers: A Moocher Manifesto

1. Helen Rubinstein, "Won't You Be My Wireless Neighbor?" *New York Times*, January 13, 2011.

Chapter 5. Addicted to OPM (Other People's Money)

1. Eric Lipton, "'Breathtaking' Waste and Fraud in Hurricane Aid," *New York Times*, June 27, 2006.

2. Tim Reid, "Katrina Response Beset by Epic Fraud," *Times of London*, February 13, 2006.

3. Ibid.

4. Spencer S. Hsu, "Waste in Katrina Response Is Cited; Housing Aid Called Inefficient in Audits," *Washington Post*, April 14, 2006.

5. Hope Yen, "GAO Probes Katrina Credit Card Bills; Audits Examine Purchases by Federal Workers for Abuse, Overpayment," Associated Press, December 27, 2005.

6. Mark Ballard, "Blanco Orders Remodeling Just After Storms," *The Advocate*, December 31, 2005.

7. Shaila Dewan, "Storm Evacuees Remain in Grip of Uncertainty," *New York Times*, December 6, 2006.

8. Matthew Philips, "A Very Late Checkout: New York's Last Katrina Evacuees Prepare to Depart (Under Duress) from the JFK Airport Holiday Inn," *New York* magazine, May 28, 2006.

9. Nicholas Confessore, "Storm Evacuees Seek Money for Vacating Queens Hotel," *New York Times,* February 4, 2006.

10. Associated Press, "Oil Spill Adds to Housing Woes for Katrina Victims in Mississippi," August 21, 2010.

11. Brendan Miniter, "LBJ's Other Quagmire: Long Before Katrina, the Welfare State Failed New Orleans's Poor," *Wall Street Journal,* September 13, 2005.

Chapter 6. Feed Me

1. Alfred Lubrano, "In City Schools, Breakfast's Now on the Principal; The Head of Each School Will Be Held Responsible for Ensuring That Students Are Well-fed," *Philadelphia Inquirer,* October 8, 2009.

2. Martha Moore, "Breakfast in Class: Fight Against Kids' Hunger Starts at School," *USA Today,* September 15, 2010.

3. Ibid.

4. Wisconsin Department of Public Instruction, "Evers Announces Winners of the Wisconsin School Breakfast Challenge," press release, December 2, 2009.

5. University of Wisconsin Extension, "Attracting More Kids to School Breakfast Programs," press release, April 9, 2010.

6. Liam Julian, "Why School Lunch Is 'Nasty!'" *Policy Review,* Oct/Nov 2010.

7. Ibid.

8. Voegeli, *Never Enough,* 249.

9. Ibid., 3.

10. Associated Press, "Congress Sends Child Nutrition Bill to Obama," December 3, 2010.

11. Moore, "Breakfast in Class."

12. "Schools Encouraged to Take the Wisconsin School Breakfast Challenge," WKOW-TV, November 11, 2008, http://www.wkow.com/Global/story.asp?S=9331100&clienttype=printable.

13. Rector, "How Poor Are America's Poor?"

14. Ibid.

15. *Wall Street Journal*, "In U.S., 14% Rely" (see chap 1, n. 15).

16. DeParle and Gebeloff, "Food Stamp Use Soars" (see chap 1, n. 14).

17. Bradley and Rector, "Confronting the Unsustainable Growth."

18. DeParle and Gebeloff, "Food Stamp Use Soars."

19. Matthew Boyle, "Universities Encouraging Students to Receive Welfare Benefits," *The Daily Caller*, December 7, 2010, http://dailycaller.com/2010/12/07/thedc-investigation-universities-encouraging-students-to-receive-welfare-benefits.

20. Jennifer Bleyer, "Hipsters on Food Stamps: They're Young, They're Broke, and They Pay for Organic Salmon with Government Subsidies. Got a Problem with That?" *Salon.com*, March 15, 2010, http://www.salon.com/life/pinched/2010/03/15/hipsters_food_stamps_pinched.

Chapter 7. Harvesting OPM

1. Alan Wirzbicki, "Is the Massachusetts Film Tax Credit Worth the Cost?" *The Angle, Boston Globe* blog, January 14, 2011, http://www.boston.com/bostonglobe/editorial_opinion/blogs/the_angle/2011/01/film_tax_credit.html.

2. Steve Leblanc, "Mass. Tax Credits Used to Cover Movie Stars' Wages," Associated Press, January 12, 2011.

3. Robert Tannenwald, "State Film Subsidies: Not Much Bang for Too Many Bucks," Center on Budget and Policy Priorities, December 9, 2010.

4. Michael Cieply, "States Weigh Cuts in Hollywood Subsidies," *New York Times*, January 19, 2011.

5. Robert Tannenwald, "State Film Subsidies."

6. John Stossel, *Give Me a Break: How I Exposed Hucksters, Cheats, and Scam Artists and Became the Scourge of the Liberal Media* (New York: HarperCollins, 2005), 140.

7. Ken Cook, "Government's Continuing Bailout of Corporate Agriculture," Environmental Working Group, May 2010.

8. Ibid.

9. Stossel, *Give Me a Break*, 141.

10. Cook, "Government's Continuing Bailout."

11. Morgan, Gaul, and Cohen, "Farm Program Pays" (see "Scenes from Moocher Nation," n. 7).

12. Ibid.

13. Gilbert M. Gaul, Sarah Cohen, and Dan Morgan, "Federal Subsidies Turn Farms into Big Business," *Washington Post*, December 21, 2006.

14. Gilbert M. Gaul, Dan Morgan, and Sarah Cohen, "No Drought Required for Federal Drought Aid," *Washington Post*, July 18, 2006.

15. Ibid.

16. Ibid.

17. Cook, "Government's Continuing Bailout."

18. Dan Morgan, Sarah Cohen, and Gilbert M. Gaul, "Growers Reap Benefits Even in Good Years," *Washington Post*, July 3, 2006.

19. Cook, "Government's Continuing Bailout."

20. Stuart Butler, "Farmer Bailouts Must Be Revised," The Heritage Foundation, April 10, 2009.

21. Morgan, Gaul, and Cohen, "Farm Program Pays."

22. Cook, "Government's Continuing Bailout."

23. Gilbert M. Gaul, "Claims Strain Federal Flood Insurance," *Washington Post*, October 11, 2005.

24. Thomas Frank, "Insurance Underwater," *USA Today*, August 26, 2010.

25. J. Scott Holladay and Jason A. Schwartz, "The Distributional Consequences of the NFIP," Institute for Policy Integrity, Policy Brief No. 7, April 2010.

26. Frank, "Flood Insurance Claims."

27. Holladay and Schwartz, "The Distributional Consequences."

28. Ibid.

29. Frank, "Flood Insurance Claims."

30. Holladay and Schwartz, "The Distributional Consequences."

Chapter 8. Crony Capitalism (Big Business at the Trough)

1. David Boaz, "The Stimulus Lobbying Frenzy," Cato Institute blog, February 2, 2009, http://www.cato-at-liberty.org/the-stimulus-lobbying-frenzy.

2. Jeffrey H. Birnbaum, "Mickey Goes to Washington," *Washington Post,* February 17, 2008.

3. *Wall Street Journal,* "The Great Misallocators: What Barack Obama and General Electric Have in Common," January 26, 2011.

4. George Stigler, "The Theory of Economic Regulation," *Bell Journal of Economics,* Spring 1971.

5. Joseph L. Bast, "Why Regulate," The Heartland Institute, policy brief, October 2010.

6. David Kocieniewski, "G.E.'s Strategies Let It Avoid Taxes Altogether," *New York Times,* March 24, 2011.

7. Timothy P. Carney, "Barack Obama and the Miracle on K Street," *Washington Examiner,* December 24, 2009.

8. Barry Ritholtz, *Bailout Nation: How Greed and Easy Money Corrupted Wall Street and Shook the World Economy* (Hoboken, N.J.: John Wiley and Sons, 2009), 273.

9. Birnbaum, "Mickey Goes to Washington."

10. Roger Yu, "Obama Signs New Law to Help Promote U.S. Tourism," *USA Today,* March 4, 2010.

11. Birnbaum, "Mickey Goes to Washington."

12. Olson, *The Rise and Decline,* 73 (see chap. 2, n. 2).

13. William Kristol, "Did You Get My Message? Congresswoman Eleanor Holmes Norton Makes a Phone Call," *Weekly Standard,* September 27, 2010.

14. Birnbaum, "Mickey Goes to Washington."

15. Timothy P. Carney, *Obamanomics* (Washington, D.C.: Regnery, 2009), 54–55.

16. James Gattuso, "Chrysler's Creditors and Offers You Can't Refuse," *The Foundry,* the Heritage Foundation, May 1, 2009.

17. Mary Williams Walsh, "Government Takes Over Delphi's Pensions," *New York Times,* July 23, 2009.

18. Ibid.

19. Carl Horowitz, "Nonunion Delphi Retired Employees Get Shaft in Auto Bailout," National Legal and Policy Center, December 31, 2009.

20. Walsh, "Government Takes Over."

21. Horowitz, "Nonunion Delphi Retired Employees."

22. Cited in "TARP Enables Big Labor Crony Capitalism Again," *The Foundry*, the Heritage Foundation, November 5, 2009.

23. *Wall Street Journal*, "Uncle Sam, Venture Capitalist," August 17, 2010.

24. Thomas Content, "ZBB Energy Says Annual Loss Widens," *Milwaukee Journal Sentinel*, September 7, 2010.

25. John Stossel, "Big Government's Cronies," RealClearPolitics, February 3, 2010.

26. Carney, *Obamanomics*, 144–45.

27. Stephen J. Dubner, "The Verdict on Cash for Clunkers: A Clunker," Freakonomics blog, *New York Times*, September 14, 2010, http://www.treakonomics.com/2010/09/14/the-verdict-on-cash-for-clunkers-a-clunker/. See Atif Mian, Amir Sufi, "The Effects of Fiscal Stimulus: Evidence from the 2009 'Cash for Clunkers' Program," NBER Working Paper No. 16351, September 2010.

28. Jeff Jacoby, "'Clunkers,' a Classic Government Folly," *Boston Globe*, September 1, 2010.

29. Stossel, *Give Me a Break*, 142.

30. Matt Purple, "Corny Capitalism," *The American Spectator*, August 2010.

31. Ibid.

32. Stossel, *Give Me a Break*, 174.

33. Dan Carney, "Dwayne's World," *Mother Jones*, July/August 1995.

34. Stossel, *Give Me a Break*, 174.

35. Darren Goode, "Oil Industry Also Sues EPA over Higher Ethanol Blend," *The Hill*, November 9, 2010.

Chapter 9. The Two Americas

1. Steven Greenhut, "How Severe Is U.S. Pension Debt? (Is California a Bellwether for Most of the Country?)," CalWatchdog, September 9, 2010, http://www.calwatchdog.com/2010/08/26/8228.

2. Fred Barnes, "The New Fat Cats: The Indefensible Pensions of Public-Sector Employees," *Weekly Standard*, May 3, 2010.

3. Luke Funke, "Audit: NJ Turnpike Wasted Millions on Perks," *Myfoxny.com*, October 20, 2010, http://www.myfoxny.com/dpp/traffic_news/audit-excessive-perks-for-nj-turnpike-employees-201010192apx.

4. *The Economist*, "Hard-Pressed American States Face a Crushing Pensions Bill," October 14, 2010. See also Robert Novy Marx and Joshua D. Rauh, "Public Pension Promises: How Big Are They and What Are They Worth?" NBER Working Paper, December 18, 2009.

5. Ed Mendel, "SB400 Pension Boost: Uncanny Forecast Unheeded," *Calpensions.com*, http://calpensions.com/2010/07/27/sb400-pension-boost-uncanny-forecast-unheeded.

6. Roger Lowenstein, "The Next Crisis: Public Pension Funds," *New York Times*, June 21, 2010.

7. Phillip Reese, "Pension Promises Threaten California Cities, Counties," *Sacramento Bee*, April 11, 2010.

8. Tim Cavanaugh, "Farewell, My Lovely: How Public Pensions Killed Progressive California," *Reason*, March 2011.

9. Brody Mullin and John D. McKinnon, "Campaign's Big Spender," *Wall Street Journal*, October 22, 2010.

10. Michael Lewis, "Beware of Greeks Bearing Bonds," *Vanity Fair*, October 1, 2010.

11. Ibid.

12. Mark Steyn, "America's Future Could Be All Greek to Us," syndicated column, February 26, 2010.

13. Peter Simon, "'Worst-Case' City School Budget Would Lay Off 700," *Buffalo News*, April 22, 2010; and Eric Randall, "Milwaukee Teachers Union Files Suit over Lack of Viagra Coverage; It Says MPS Is Discriminating Against Male Employees," *Milwaukee Journal Sentinel*, August 6, 2010.

14. Dennis Cauchon, "More Federal Workers' Pay Tops $150,000," *USA Today*, November 10, 2010.

15. Dennis Cauchon, "For Feds, More Get 6-Figure Salaries," *USA Today*, December 11, 2009.

16. Cauchon, "Federal Workers Earning Double" (see chap. 1, n. 13).

17. Dennis Cauchon, "Federal Pay Ahead of Private Industry," *USA Today,* March 4, 2010.

18. *Washington Examiner,* "Bonus Bonanza for Federal Workers," June 16, 2010.

19. *Washington Times,* "Gov't Workers Feel No Economic Pain," March 11, 2010.

20. Reuters, "Study: 47% of Boomers Don't Have Enough to Retire," July 13, 2010.

21. Greenhut, "How Severe."

22. Arnold Schwarzenegger, "Public Pensions and Our Fiscal Future," *Wall Street Journal,* August 27, 2010.

23. Rich Karlgaard, "The Millionaire Cop Next Door," *Forbes,* June 1, 2010.

24. Susan Schulman, "No Crime Too Big to Take Away a Public Pension," *Buffalo News,* July 7, 2010.

25. *NBCNewYork.com,* "FDNY Marathoner Received $86K Disability Pension for Asthma," July 6, 2010, http://www.nbcnewyork.com/news/local/FDNY-Marathoner-Received-Disability-Pension-for-Asthma-97859344.html.

26. Mary Williams Walsh and Amy Schoenfeld, "Padded Pensions Add to New York Fiscal Woes," *New York Times,* May 20, 2010.

27. Bob Sullivan, "Does Your City Manager Earn $800,000?" *MSNBC.com,* the Red Tape Chronicles, September 24, 2010, http://redtape.msnbc.msn.com/_news/2010/09/24/6345545-does-your-city-manager-earn-800000.

28. Bob Sullivan, "20 Government Workers with Super-Sized Pay," *MSNBC.com,* the Red Tape Chronicles, October 5, 2010, http://redtape.msnbc.msn.com/_news/2010/10/05/6345539-20-government-workers-with-super-sized-pay.

29. John Rogers, "Calif. Town Outraged to Learn of Officials' Pay," Associated Press, July 23, 2010.

30. Joseph Ryan, "$472,255 to Run a Town of 20,000; Village Officials Can't Explain Why Roy McCampbell Was Paid So Much to Run Bellwood," *Chicago Tribune,* June 29, 2010.

31. Joseph Ryan, "Park District Pension Ploy Pays Off Handsomely; Park Executives in Highland Park Collected Huge Salaries, Bonuses—Even a Free SUV—During Height of Recession," *Chicago Tribune,* July 31, 2010.

32. Luke Funke, "Audit: NJ Turnpike Wasted Millions on Perks," *Myfoxny. com,* October 20, 2010, http://www.myfoxny.com/dpp/traffic_news/ audit-excessive-perks-for-nj-turnpike-employees-201010192apx.

33. Steve Schultze, "Milwaukee County Pension Backdrops Surge; Payouts to County Retirees at Highest Level in Six Years," *Milwaukee Journal Sentinel,* October 1, 2010.

34. Lucy Morgan, "Double Dipping Rises Despite Outrage," *St. Petersburg Times,* December 28, 2008.

35. Ibid.

36. Sullivan, "20 Government Workers."

37. Morgan, "Double Dipping Rises."

38. Diane Rado and Duaa Eldeib, "Rules Let Educators Cross State Lines to Get Pensions Along with Salaries," *Chicago Tribune,* January 30, 2011.

39. Nick Perry and Justin Mayo, "Retired, Then Rehired: How College Workers Use Loophole to Boost Pay," *Seattle Times,* June 26, 2010.

40. Ryan Blethen, "Washington Legislature Must Stop Double-Dipping by State Pensioners," *Seattle Times,* July 6, 2010.

41. Bill Bush, "School Employees Can Get Paid Twice," *Columbus Dispatch,* September 20, 2009.

42. *The Pilot* (North Carolina), "The Poster Child of Pension Excess," June 20, 2010.

43. Bureau of Labor Statistics, "Compensation and Working Conditions," http://www.bls.gov/iif/oshwc/cfar0020.pdf, and "Number of Fatal Work Injuries (1992–2008)," http://www.bls.gov/iif/oshwc/cfoi/cfch0007 .pdf; *Boston.com,* "Americans' 10 Most Dangerous Jobs," http://www .boston.com/jobs/galleries/dangerous_jobs_2007; and Matt Kirdahy, "America's Most Dangerous Jobs," *Forbes.com,* http://www.forbes .com/2008/08/25/dangerous-jobs-fishing-lead-careers-cx_mk _0825danger.html.

44. Greenhut, "How Severe."

45. Mattie Corrao, "Cost of Government Day Finally Arrives on August 19, 2010," Americans for Tax Reform, August 19, 2010.

46. Rev. Jesse Jackson Sr., "Injustices, from Memphis to Madison," *Capital Times,* April 1, 2011.

47. The MacIver Institute, "Wisconsin Fiscal Crisis Fast Facts," March 2011, http://maciverinstitute.com/wp-content/uploads/2011/03/WI_Fiscal_Crisis_Fast_Facts.pdf.

48. Ianthe Jean Dugan, "Public Employees Rush to Retire," *Wall Street Journal,* March 23, 2011.

49. Quoted in Jeff Jacoby, "Union 'Rights' That Aren't," *Boston Globe,* March 2, 2011; FDR's letter to Luther C. Steward, president of the National Federation of Federal Employees, August 16, 1937. Meany quote at http://www.conservativeblog.org/amyridenour/2011/2/24/afl-cio-president-george-meany-on-public-sector-unions.html.

50. Jacoby, "Union 'Rights.'"

51. Amy Hetzner, "More Districts Now Could Drop Insurance Arm of Teachers Union," *Milwaukee Journal Sentinel,* March 13, 2011.

52. WLUK, "140 Teacher Retirement Requests Approved," Green Bay, March 3, 2011.

53. Adam Rodewald, "Union Concessions Would Save Oshkosh District at Least $4 Million with Renegotiated Contracts," *Oshkosh Northwestern,* March 18, 2011.

54. Christian Schneider, "Why He Did It," *WI Magazine,* March 2011.

55. Bill Glauber, "Indiana Governor Set the Blueprint," *Milwaukee Journal Sentinel,* March 27, 2011.

Lessons in Moral Hazard

1. Allard E. Dembe and Leslie I. Boden, "Moral Hazard: A Question of Morality," *New Solutions* 10, no. 3 (2000): 257–79.

Chapter 10. Mortgage Madness

1. Ritholtz, *Bailout Nation,* 128 (see chap. 8, n. 8).

2. Ibid., 120.

3. Arnold Kling, "The Fantasy Testimony Continues," Library of Economics and Liberty, October 14, 2008.

4. Ritholtz, *Bailout Nation*, 122.

5. Ibid., 121.

6. Charles Duhigg, "At Freddie Mac, Chief Discarded Warning Sign," *New York Times*, August 5, 2008.

7. Ibid.

8. Carol D. Leonnig, "How HUD Mortgage Policy Fed the Crisis; Subprime Loans Labeled 'Affordable,'" *Washington Post*, June 10, 2008.

9. Ibid.

10. Ibid.

11. *The Foundry*, "The Left Has Learned Nothing from Fannie/Freddie Failure," the Heritage Foundation, September 19, 2008.

12. J. Taylor Rushing and Jim Snyder, "The Debate over Fannie and Freddie's Future Under Way," *The Hill*, September 18, 2008.

13. Kevin Park, "Subprime Lending and the Community Reinvestment Act," Joint Center for Housing Studies, Harvard University, November 2008.

14. Howard Husock, "The Trillion-Dollar Bank Shakedown That Bodes Ill for Cities," *City Journal*, Winter 2000.

15. Ibid.

16. Ibid.

17. *The Foundry*, "Fannie and Freddie Failure Forever," the Heritage Foundation, May 6, 2010.

18. Binyamin Appelbaum, Carol D. Leonnig, and David S. Hilzenrath, "How Washington Failed to Rein in Fannie, Freddie: As Profits Grew, Firms Used Their Power to Mask Peril," *Washington Post*, September 14, 2008.

19. Leonnig, "How HUD Mortgage Policy."

Chapter 11. Bailouts for Idiots
(How to Make Out Big by Screwing Up)

1. Congressional Oversight Committee, "Congressional Oversight Panel Examines AIG Rescue and Its Impact on Markets," June 10, 2010.

2. Ritholtz, *Bailout Nation*, 217.

3. Marcus Baram, "Judge Richard Posner Questions His Free-Market Faith in 'A Failure of Capitalism,'" *Huffington Post*, April 20, 2009, http://www.huffingtonpost.com/2009/04/20/judge-richard-posner -disc_n_188950.html.

4. Ritholtz, *Bailout Nation*, 205.

5. Carney, *Obamanomics*, 163 (see chap. 8, n. 15).

6. Gretchen Morgenson and Louise Story, "Testy Conflict with Goldman Helped Push AIG to Edge," *New York Times*, February 7, 2010.

7. Hagan, "Tenacious G" (see "Scenes from Moocher Nation," n. 1).

8. Congressional Oversight Committee, "Congressional Oversight."

9. Hagan, "Tenacious G."

10. Carney, *Obamanomics*, 165.

11. Louise Story and Gretchen Morgenson, "In U.S. Bailout of A.I.G., Forgiveness for Big Banks," *New York Times*, June 29, 2010.

12. Ibid.

13. Congressional Oversight Committee, "Congressional Oversight."

14. Story and Morgenson, "In U.S. Bailout."

15. Congressional Oversight Committee, "Congressional Oversight."

16. Ibid.

17. Ibid.

18. Ibid.

19. Graham Bowley, "With Big Profit, Goldman Sees Big Payday Ahead," *New York Times*, July 15, 2009.

Chapter 12. Walk Away from Your Mortgage!

1. David Streitfeld, "Owners Stop Paying Mortgages, and Stop Fretting," *New York Times*, May 13, 2010.

2. Ibid.

3. Cassy Fiano, "Old and Busted: Paying Your Mortgage. New Hotness: Living in Foreclosure Without Paying Anything," *HotAir.com*, June 1, 2010, http://www.cassyfiano.com/2010/06/old-and-busted-paying-your

-mortgage-new-hotness-living-in-foreclosure-without-paying-any thing.

4. Brett Arends, "When It's OK to Walk Away from Your Home," *Wall Street Journal,* February 26, 2010.

5. Roger Lowenstein, "Walk Away from Your Mortgage!" *New York Times Magazine,* January 10, 2010.

6. White, "Underwater and Not Walking Away" (see chap. 1, n. 11).

7. Luigi Guiso, Paola Sapienza, and Luigi Zingales, "Moral and Social Constraints to Strategic Default on Mortgages," NBER Working Paper No. 15145, July 2009.

8. White, "Underwater and Not Walking Away."

9. Ibid.

10. Guiso, Sapienza, and Zingales, "Moral and Social Constraints."

Chapter 13. No, They Didn't Learn Anything

1. Andrew Haughwout, Ebiere Okah, and Joseph Tracy, "Second Chances: Subprime Mortgage Modification and Re-Default," Federal Reserve Bank of New York, Staff Report no. 417, December 2009, revised August 2010. See also David Streitfeld, "Defaults Rise in Loan Modification Program," *New York Times,* April 14, 2010.

2. Arthur Delaney and Shahien Nasiripour, "Extend and Pretend," *Huffington Post,* August 8, 2010, http://www.huffingtonpost.com/2010/08/04/extend-and-pretend-the-ob_n_668609.html.

3. John Leland, "New Program for Buyers, with No Money Down," *New York Times,* September 4, 2010.

4. Diana Olick, "Home Ownership: Do You Really Need Skin in the Game?" *CNBC.com,* September 10, 2010, http://www.cnbc.com/id/39097208/Home_Ownership_Do_You_Really_Need_Skin_in_the_Game.

5. Leland, "New Program for Buyers."

6. David Streitfeld, "A Bold U.S. Plan to Help Struggling Homeowners," *New York Times,* March 26, 2010.

7. Department of the Treasury, "Housing Program Enhancements Offer Additional Options for Struggling Homeowners," press release, March 26, 2010.

8. Keith Hennessey, "Should Taxpayers Subsidize Underwater Home-owners?," blog posting, March 26, 2010, http://keithhennessey.com/2010/03/26/underwater.

9. Larry Kudlow, "TARP-ing the Upper Class Is an Outrage," *National Review Online*, March 29, 2010, http://finance.townhall.com/columnists/larrykudlow/2010/03/29/tarp-ing_the_upper_class_is_an_outrage.

10. Hennessey, "Should Taxpayers Subsidize."

Chapter 14. The Bank of Mom and Dad

1. Charles J. Sykes, *50 Rules Kids Won't Learn in School* (New York: St. Martin's Press, 2007), 79.

2. Frank F. Furstenberg, Sheela Kennedy, Vonnie C. McLoyd et al., "Growing Up Is Harder to Do," *Contexts*, American Sociological Association, Summer 2004.

3. Frank F. Furstenberg, Jr., Rubén G. Rumbaut, and Richard A. Settersten, Jr., "On the Frontier of Adulthood: Emerging Themes and New Directions," Network on Transitions to Adulthood, policy brief, October 2004, issue 1.

4. Ted Mouw, "The Effect of Timing and Sequence of Choices on Young Adults' Futures," Network on Transitions to Adulthood, policy brief, October 2004, issue 8.

5. Robert Schoeni and Karen Ross, "Family Support During the Transition to Adulthood," Network on Transitions to Adulthood, policy brief, October 2004, issue 12.

6. Anna Bahney, "The Bank of Mom and Dad," *New York Times*, April 20, 2006.

7. Schoeni and Ross, "Family Support."

8. Bahney, "The Bank of Mom and Dad."

Chapter 15. Middle-Class Suckers

1. Glenn Grothman, "The Government's Message to America: Don't Get Married," undated, Office of Wisconsin State Senator Glenn Grothman.

2. Public Service Loan Forgiveness (PSLF), Federal Student Aid website, http://studentaid.ed.gov/PORTALSWebApp/students/english/PSF.jsp; and "Income-Based Repayment Plan," http://studentaid.ed.gov/PORTALSWebApp/students/english/IBRPlan.jsp.

3. The Kaiser Family Foundation Health Reform subsidy calculator: http://healthreform.kff.org/SubsidyCalculator.aspx.

4. Janet Novack and Stephanie Fitch, "When Work Doesn't Pay for the Middle Class," *Forbes,* October 5, 2009.

5. Ibid.

6. Public Service Loan Forgiveness.

7. Nancy K. Cauthen, "When Work Doesn't Pay; What Every Policymaker Should Know," NCCP, June 2006.

8. Grothman, "The Government's Message."

9. Cauthen, "When Work Doesn't Pay."

10. Lipton, " 'Breathtaking' Waste and Fraud" (see chap. 5, n. 1).

11. The Center on Budget and Policy Priorities, "The Earned Income Tax Credit," December 4, 2009.

12. Ibid.

13. U.S. Government Accountability Office, "Means-Tested Programs: Report to the Ranking Minority Member, Committee on the Budget, House of Representatives," March 2005.

14. Novack and Fitch, "When Work Doesn't Pay."

15. Kaiser Family Foundation subsidy calculator.

16. Scott Gottlieb, "O's Middle-Class Squeeze," *New York Post,* March 18, 2010.

Chapter 16. Why Get a Job?

1. Jaclyn Trop, "Landscapers Find Workers Choosing Jobless Pay," *Detroit News,* May 10, 2010.

2. Ibid.

3. Cited in Alan Reynolds, "The 'Stimulus' for Unemployment," *New York Post,* November 17, 2009.

4. Lawrence H. Summers, "Unemployment," *The Concise Encyclopedia of Economics,* http://www.econlib.org/library/Enc/Unemployment.html. See also James M. Poterba and Lawrence H. Summers, "Unemployment Benefits, Labor Market Transitions, and Spurious Flows: A Multinational Logit Model with Errors in Classification," NBER Working Paper No. 4434, September 1995; Martin Feldstein, "The Economics of

the New Unemployment," *Public Interest* 33 (Fall 1973): 3–42; Martin Feldstein, "Why Is Productivity Growing Faster?" NBER Working Paper no. 9530, March 2003; Robert Hall, "Employment Fluctuations and Wage Rigidity," Brookings Papers on Economic Activity 1 (1980): 91–141; Lawrence H. Summers, *Understanding Unemployment* (Cambridge, Mass.: MIT Press, 1990); Lawrence H. Summers, "Why Is the Unemployment Rate So Very High Near Full Employment?" Brookings Papers on Economic Activity 2 (1986): 339–83; and Lawrence H. Summers and Kim B. Clark, "Labor Market Dynamics and Unemployment: A Reconsideration," Brookings Papers on Economic Activity 1 (1979): 13–60.

5. Alan B. Krueger and Bruce D. Meyer, "Labor Supply Effects of Social Insurance," National Bureau of Economic Research, February 2002.

6. Cited in Reynolds, "The 'Stimulus' for Unemployment."

7. Robert Barro, "The Folly of Subsidizing Unemployment," *Wall Street Journal*, August 30, 2010.

Chapter 17. Mooching Off the Kids

1. Jeremy Pelzer, "Al Simpson Speaks Out Against Debt Committee Critics, Political Climate," *Casper Star-Tribune*, November 24, 2010.

2. Nick Gillespie and Veronique de Rugy, "The 19 Percent Solution: How to Balance the Budget without Increasing Taxes," *Reason*, March 2011.

3. The Heritage Foundation, "2010 Budget Chart Book," Washington, D.C., 2010. http://www.heritage.org/budgetchartbook/PDF/All-Budget-chart-book-2010.pdf.

4. Riedl, "Federal Spending" (see chap. 1, n. 19).

5. Paul Ryan and Jeb Hensarling, "Big Government Debt Mortgages Our Children's Future," *Washington Examiner*, June 21, 2010.

6. "The Next Generation's Debt Burden," House Republican conference based on CBO projections, http://www.gop.gov/policy-news/10/08/24/the-next-generations-debt-burden.

7. Paul Krugman, "Fiscal Scare Tactics," *New York Times*, February 5, 2010.

8. Ibid.

9. *Scrivener.net,* "Krugman Versus Krugman on Deficits and Debt—Who

Can You Believe?" August 29, 2009, http://blog.scrivener.net/2009/08/krugman-versus-krugman-on-deficits-and.html.

10. Paul Krugman, "A Fiscal Train Wreck," *New York Times,* March 11, 2003.

11. Cindy Perman, "Dying with Debt: A Dirty Little Retirement Secret," *USA Today,* November 22, 2010.

12. Christopher Buckley, *Boomsday* (New York: Twelve, Hatchett Book Group, 2007), ff.

13. Riedl, "Federal Spending."

14. Robert J. Samuelson, "A Rail Boondoggle, Moving at High Speed," *Newsweek,* August 24, 2009; also Robert J. Samuelson, "High-Speed Pork: Why Fast Trains Are a Waste of Money," *Newsweek,* October 29, 2010.

15. Riedl, "Federal Spending."

16. Ibid.

Chapter 18. We're All from Starnesville Now

1. Ayn Rand, *Atlas Shrugged* (New York: Dutton, 1992), 660–72.

2. Ibid., 660–61.

3. Ibid., 662.

4. Ibid.

5. Ibid., 665.

6. Ibid., 323.

7. Ibid., 666.

8. Ibid., 666–67.

9. Ibid., 667.

10. Ibid., 663–64.

11. Ibid., 309.

12. Ibid., 310.

Chapter 19. What's Fair?

1. Robert Nozick, *Anarchy, State, and Utopia* (New York: Basic Books, 1974), 168–72.

2. Ibid., 163.

3. Ibid., 161.

4. Ibid., 160.

5. Voegeli, *Never Enough,* 102–3 (see chap. 1, n. 22).

6. John Rawls, *A Theory of Justice* (Cambridge, Mass.: Harvard University Press, 1971), 64.

7. Ibid., 103–4.

8. Schmidtz, *Elements of Justice,* 60 (see chap. 1, n. 2).

9. Ibid.

10. Rich Lowry, "Bourgeois Dignity & the Miracle of the Modern World," *RealClearPolitics.com,* December 3, 2010, http://www.realclearpolitics .com/articles/2010/12/03/innovation__the_miracle_of_the_modern_ world_108143.html.

11. Deirdre McCloskey, *Bourgeois Dignity: Why Economics Can't Explain the Modern World* (Chicago: University of Chicago Press, 2010), 1.

12. Aristotle, *Politics* 2. 3. 1261b, translated by Benjamin Jowett as *The Politics of Aristotle: Translated into English with Introduction, Marginal Analysis, Essays, Notes and Indices* (Oxford: Clarendon Press, 1885), vol. 1 of 2.

Chapter 20. Step Away from the Trough

1. Kelly L. Ross, "Rent-Seeking, Public Choice, and the Prisoner's Dilemma," www.friesian.com/rent.htm, http://www.roadmap.republicans .budget.house.gov.

2. Chris Edwards, "A Plan to Cut Spending and Balance the Federal Budget," Cato Institute, November 2010.

3. Paul Ryan, "A Roadmap for America's Future," Budget Committee Republicans, House of Representatives, Washington, D.C., 2010. http:// www.roadmap.republicans.budget.house.gov/.

4. Olson, *The Rise and Decline,* 73 (see chap. 2, n. 2).

5. George Lightbourn, "It's Morning Again in Wisconsin," *WI Magazine,* Fall 2010.

Index